THE LEADER'S CHOICE

Bridging the Leadership Gap in an
Uncertain World and Winning

Jason Roncoroni and Zebrina Warner

www.zerosixgroup.com

To those who have the courage to step onto the field and leave everything they have for everyone else.

CONTENTS

Introduction: The Bridge

The romantic, spendthrift moral act is ultimately the practical one - the practical, expedient cozy-dog move is the one that comes to grief. If it comes to a choice between being a good soldier and a good human being - try to be a good human being.[1]

What does it take to be an effective leader? Companies invest over $14 billion a year to answer this elusive question.[2] Given the size of that investment, the market for executive development has been flooded with consultants, coaches, and business schools trying to teach you how to lead. Along the way, most executive education opportunities have become extensions of MBA programs reinforcing functional-based skill sets instead of the behavioral qualities for effective leadership.[3] From that approach, we validate the quality of leadership development based on business metrics like profitability. Numbers matter. We presume that the companies with a better bottom line have better leaders.

Numbers provide a practical, expedient assessment for leadership effectiveness, and if we assume stable economic, political, and social conditions, the math works. The business calculus can predict cause and effect. You just need to plug the right numbers into the right equation. Unfortunately, survey data shows that today's businesses are required to reinvent and transform themselves at an unprecedented pace.[4] What worked yesterday won't necessarily work today, and what works today might be irrelevant tomorrow. Change is the new state of being. We don't know the right equations or factors to do the math. When you can't calculate the business metrics, how do you measure leadership? When the numbers no longer correlate in today's uncertain world, the otherwise practical, expedient move comes to grief.

Volatility, uncertainty, complexity, and ambiguity (VUCA) describes the political, economic, and social state of play in the 21st century. Already in the new millennium we've experienced the reach of global terrorism, catastrophic weather events, economic instability, political polarization, social unrest, and - of course - the coronavirus pandemic. On the positive side, we've also benefited from innovations like artificial intelligence, quantum computing, and digital commerce. Given the scope and scale of disruptive events since the turn of the century, how do we prepare today's leaders for tomorrow's unknown challenges?

Let's start with the basics. Leadership is about human interaction. It describes the confidence to motivate others toward a positive outcome, the competence to discover and implement creative solutions, and the commitment to support the people as they achieve those solutions. The leadership necessary to thrive and win in today's uncertain world has little to do with managing people to accomplish a *specific* mission and more to do with unleashing their potential to accomplish *any* mission. Leadership isn't about numbers. It's about people.

The quote at the beginning of this introduction comes from Anton Myrer's *Once an Eagle*, a best-selling novel originally published in 1968. Inside the military community, this is one of the few works of fiction found on almost every military leader's reading list. For more than half a century, leaders have been sharing this story to showcase the most important choice for every military leader: To be a good soldier or a good human being.

There is a hidden riddle in that dilemma. A good soldier might dutifully follow orders, but good soldiers are not necessarily good people. Naked ambition has its limitations and comes at a cost. Instead, focus on the character and those related qualities to be the best version of yourself. The best people are *always* the best soldiers and military leaders. Make better people, and you'll have the best leaders. That's the point. Compassion is the leader's currency. The *moral* act is one where you consider the people first. It becomes *spendthrift* when you commit everything you've got to make them better. **The spendthrift moral act is where leaders choose their people before anything else - including themselves.** This is the leader's choice, and if you want to win in today's world, it's the only practical one.

How do we develop leaders with the confidence, competence, and commitment to choose the people before business metrics? How do we coach, teach, and mentor future leaders to prioritize the people above themselves? We believe this is an area where civilian society can learn from the military. From the first day of service on active duty, the military forges an identity as a leader so that regardless of the situation, service members have the confidence, competence, and commitment to lead. Since the turn of the century, we've challenged military leaders to go anywhere in the world in the most volatile, uncertain, complex, ambiguous, and dangerous environments with the highest stakes. Their only requirement has been to win regardless of the limitations or constraints. Time and again, they've found a way to do that by harnessing the full potential of everyone on the team. From the perspective of today's military leader, the people are the mission.

Throughout our history, leadership has been the greatest contribution that the military profession offers society through its veterans. Unfortunately, veterans are a disappearing segment of our population and a shrinking minority in the workforce. Therefore, our challenge is to capture the best practices of military leadership for nonmilitary applications. Building that bridge between the military experience and civilian society is the purpose of this book. In addition to describing how military leaders succeed in the modern VUCA reality, we will outline the Align, Develop, Apply, Process, and Transform (ADAPT) Framework using the foundation of emotional intelligence and behavioral science to inspire leaders, including you, in any industry to win in today's uncertain world.

Leadership is not a cognitive skill. It is not enough just to know how to lead. Inspiring another human being to willingly follow you requires emotional intention and personal will. You have to want this responsibility. It is a discipline requiring self-awareness, wisdom, and practice. In every leader's journey, there comes a time when that intention and will are tested. It normally occurs when you aren't expecting it, the conditions are desperate, and you feel dangerously vulnerable. Unfortunately, these are also the very moments when others are counting on you the most. The choices you make and how you influence the outcome will define your effectiveness as a leader. So let's begin by exploring what it means to face that leadership moment.

1 | FACING THE LEADERSHIP MOMENT

Once more unto the breach, dear friends, once more . . .
In peace there's nothing so becomes a man
As modest stillness and humility:
But when the blast of war blows in our ears,
Then imitate the action of the tiger;
Stiffen the sinews, summon up the blood,
Disguise fair nature with hard-favour'd rage;
Then lend the eye a terrible aspect;
Let pry through the portage of the head
Like the brass cannon; let the brow o'erwhelm it
As fearfully as doth a galled rock
O'erhang and jutty his confounded base,
Swill'd with the wild and wasteful ocean.
Now set the teeth and stretch the nostril wide,
Hold hard the breath and bend up every spirit
To his full height.

-   William Shakespeare's "Henry V Act 3 Scene 1"

"Deceased."

It was an abrupt reply, and a word I wasn't ready to process. We just spent four hours scouring the desolate landscape in southern Afghanistan only to discover our missing helicopter and crew less than a mile from the approach end of the secure boundary of Kandahar Airfield. The sun was beginning to set when we found the OH-58D Kiowa Warrior. The crew departed several hours earlier on a routine maintenance test flight. This should have been an easy mission, but that's what makes the nature of war so sinister. Even in combat, accidents still happened.

I was the executive officer for our task force. At the time, I was in the operations center and sitting next to the commander. We were monitoring the ongoing search activities by way of the radio traffic broadcast through a speaker system while watching live video feeds from unmanned aircraft on big screen televisions mounted toward the front of the room. The rightmost television had the live video of the crash site. The resolution was remarkably clear, but the crash was so severe I couldn't recognize a rotor blade, tail mast, or anything else resembling a helicopter.

There was an impending sense of dread rising from the pit of my stomach as I watched the medics enter our field of view and approach what remained of the aircraft. I feared the worst, but there wasn't a post-crash fire. I was somewhat hopeful when I saw two stretchers with our soldiers emerge from the wreckage. For a fleeting moment, I thought that maybe Chief Warrant Officer James Carter (JC) and Specialist Andre McNair had survived. From the command center, we impatiently pressed the medics for an update on the status of the crew, and their one word reply extinguished that hope.

This was my second combat tour to Afghanistan, but the first time I experienced the death of a soldier from my unit. I was an army major serving with Task Force Eagle Assault, a battalion sized aviation unit deployed to southern Afghanistan as part of Operation Enduring Freedom. Our task force consisted of thirty-five helicopters and nearly 700 soldiers from the 101st Airborne Division.

Our unit originated from Fort Campbell, Kentucky, but in 2008, Kandahar, Afghanistan was the place we called home.

The command center on Kandahar Airfield served as the base of operations for our task force. It was housed inside a hastily constructed wood structure surrounded by concrete barriers adjacent to helicopter parking on the south side of the flight line. In addition to the base of operations, the headquarters building consisted of a series of interconnected rooms for mission planning, a conference room for operational briefings, and living areas for myself and the other senior leaders in the battalion. From the outside, our headquarters looked like something the neighborhood kids would assemble using refuse from a construction site. From the inside, our operations center housed the most technologically advanced communications and digital systems in the world. From this building, our task force coordinated and managed all U.S. conventional army aviation operations across southern and western Afghanistan.

Given the scope of our mission, the command center was always busy. We supported missions around the clock over a geographical area the size of Colorado. When we first arrived in Afghanistan, the constant flurry of activity was overwhelming. As we approached the midpoint of our yearlong tour, we became relatively inoculated to the ongoing symphony of operations orchestrated through our operations center. We acclimated to a new normal. Reports of troops in contact, an urgent MEDEVAC request, or surface to air engagements targeting our aircraft hardly caught my attention, but when I heard the word "deceased" echo from the radio, I felt like I had been sucker punched in the stomach.

Aviation is a dangerous business - especially in a place like Afghanistan. Since our task force arrived six months earlier, we had our share of entanglements with both the enemy and the harsh environment. On more than a few occasions, helicopters returned to the airfield scarred with bullet holes or damaged from difficult landings on unforgiving terrain. Up to this point, our crews remained unscathed. We even developed a bit of a swagger. On this particular afternoon, I was reminded of just how vulnerable we were to the hazards of flying helicopters in this forgotten part of the world. After all, this was the volatile, uncertain, complex, and often ambiguous environment of Afghanistan.

I thought I was prepared for this moment. Unfortunately, you never really know how you might respond until it happens. Moreover, I never would have guessed JC would be our first casualty. He was one of our most experienced and capable pilots. Several months later, an accident investigation concluded that a combination of factors caused the rotor system to slow to a near stop causing the helicopter to fall from the sky. Accidents are preventable. This should not have happened - especially with one of our best pilots on the controls. If this kind of thing could happen to the best of us, what did that suggest for the rest of us?

I was shocked, but I wasn't alone. When the word "deceased" echoed through the command center, everything came to a screeching halt. For a brief time, the entire room fell silent. That silence was broken when the commander kicked a table and stormed out of the room. From the corner of my eye, I watched him disappear into the adjoining conference room. He had some difficult calls to make. That was his responsibility. As the second in command, handling this room was going to be my responsibility.

JC was beloved by the entire task force. We all knew this forty-two year old husband and father from Alabama as an extremely competent, charismatic maintenance pilot. He was a respected leader, and our soldiers trusted him. So did I. The commander recently elevated him to the position of production control officer. This made him responsible for managing the aircraft maintenance across our task force. It was an important job requiring a combination of leadership and technical expertise. JC was the right person for the job. The thought of losing any soldier on a deployment is hard, but nobody was prepared to lose someone like him.

Specialist McNair, the other "deceased" soldier, was much younger and lesser known throughout our task force. Andre was only twenty years old. Unlike JC, he was relatively new to the army. The war in Afghanistan started before he had even entered high school. For my part, I believed leaders had an obligation to look after the younger soldiers. This was our sacred responsibility to the sons and daughters of our nation, so I couldn't help but feel like we had failed in our mission.

There was a lot going on in my head at the time. I kept staring at the television as if waiting for some instructions about how to handle this situation to magically appear. Behind where I was sitting, I felt the presence of a crowd that began assembling hours earlier when we initially lost contact with the aircraft. Once the commander left, I felt the weight of those eyes upon me.

Normally, only mission-essential personnel were allowed inside the command center. At any given time on an average day, the command center was occupied by no more than ten to twelve soldiers. This was not an average day. When I finally stood and turned to face the crowd, I noticed that the entire room was filled to capacity. There were at least thirty soldiers stuffed three rows deep against the walls surrounding the room. The overflow just outside the entrance had twice that number of people waiting for updates. Tragedy has a way of attracting an audience. This is particularly true when that tragedy involves a beloved leader like JC.

JC was a good man. That's what made him a great leader. I enjoyed being around JC because he was always upbeat and positive. He had a great sense of humor and a way of making soldiers laugh during difficult times. Every day he would drive up and down the flight line to check on the mechanics working on helicopters in the blistering heat. I could see his smiling face as I stood before the men and women in this room. I felt the weight of their stares, and the only thing I knew for sure in that moment was that I didn't want to lose anyone else.

That urgency provided the clarity I needed. My focus was on the people. Discipline is important for soldiers, but confidence is an imperative for combat aviators. In war, death has many allies. For an aviation unit, a momentary lack of concentration or attention to detail has devastating consequences. This was especially true in an environment like Afghanistan. Yes, we were shaken, but at our core, I believed these people were among the best soldiers and aviators in our army. My immediate task was to restore that discipline and confidence.

For better or worse, we didn't have time to catch our breath. There are no timeouts in combat. We had a number of helicopters out supporting other missions, and we had more scheduled to fly through the night and into the next day. As the main provider for rotary wing aviation in southern Afghanistan, too many units from more than three-dozen nations were counting on us. Roads were limited and often covered with improvised explosive devices. With the noted exception of a handful of aircraft from coalition partners, we were the only alternative. Demand was always high. We had to keep flying. The relentless pace would continue because we didn't have another choice. Lives were always at stake, but I believed our soldiers were up to this challenge.

It wasn't enough for me to believe in this team, they had to believe in themselves. Especially now. I focused them on the mission related things I knew they could do. We had planned for and rehearsed this contingency. I began by directing the battle captain - the officer in charge of the command center - to execute the pre-planned procedures for a downed aircraft and death of a soldier. We developed a hasty plan to recover the helicopter wreckage from the crash site. Finally, I requested a detailed review of the next day's missions.

After the initial set of instructions, I felt an obligation to address the team. In many ways, we were like a family. I reminded them of our reputation. We were aviators from the 101st Airborne Division - the home of the air assault. Because we loved our fallen brothers, we needed to do our jobs with the discipline, competence, and professionalism worthy of their sacrifice. It wasn't much of a motivational speech, but it was authentic. Under the circumstances, it was the best that I could do. Once I was finished talking, the crowd began to disperse, and the command center resumed operations.

I wanted to sprint out of the room. I felt like I was suffocating. As I left the building, I walked past several groups of soldiers huddled together, grieving for their fallen comrades. That certainly didn't help. I tried not to notice them. A part of me wanted to say something, but I thought the best thing I could do was to leave them alone. For the sake of the team, I had to maintain my composure. I knew it was going to be a long night.

I accompanied the flight surgeon to the morgue to process the remains of our fallen. The morgue was adjacent to the hospital on Kandahar Airfield about a mile away from our headquarters building. This was my first trip to the morgue, so I wasn't sure what to expect. By the time we arrived, JC and Andre were lying on tables next to one another in the center of a brightly lit room. There was an overwhelming stench of petroleum from the aircraft fluids that had soaked their uniforms. I found it hard to look at our soldiers, but I also found it hard to look away. By the severity of their injuries, I could tell their death was both immediate and catastrophic. I never professed to be a religious man, but in that moment, I was certainly praying for strength.

As we were leaving, we were able to intercept the commander as he was about to enter. I respected his impulse. We were lucky to have him as a commander. He had always gone out of his way for our unit, but he didn't need to go into that room. He didn't need to see that. There was nothing he could do for JC or Andre, and he had a greater responsibility to the rest of the team. His job was to lead the battalion through this difficult time. My job was to help him do that.

We conducted the operational update once everyone returned to the command center. We followed the standard agenda as if nothing happened. Once complete, I took some time to check-in with each soldier on duty at the time. I knew they could do their jobs. That wasn't the issue. I needed to know they were okay. I didn't want any distractions that might contribute to another accident. Our ability to handle the next twelve hours depended on it.

It was well after midnight before things started to slow down. Back at Fort Campbell, a casualty notification officer was being tasked to deliver the fateful news to the families. We would carry two, flag draped coffins into the back of an awaiting air force jet for JC and Andre's final trip home. Bagpipes would play "Amazing Grace" at an airfield ceremony to commemorate our fallen. We would sound taps at a memorial service and confer awards posthumously. The army would initiate an investigation that would explain why this happened and send us a replacement helicopter. Even death had a routine in Afghanistan. We simply followed the script.

The war continued as the sun began to rise for a new day. Along the flight line, aircraft engines came to life and rotors began to turn for the next day's missions. Almost on cue, the air raid sirens on Kandahar sounded the warning for another rocket attack. We resumed our version of normal.

This was one of the worst days of my life. What made it so difficult was the fact that I had to be at my best. Combat exposes your deepest vulnerabilities.

Despite years of training and experience, I didn't feel like I was ready to stand in that room with everyone's eyes upon me - looking for answers I just didn't have. What I learned from that challenge was that I found confidence and faith to persevere from the competence and commitment of our team. In combat - the extreme limit of the human condition - soldiers don't fight for mission or country. They fight for each other. That's the riddle of the spendthrift moral act. True power to win comes from the people.

Chances are you've been the beneficiary of the spendthrift moral act. Think about a time when a coach pulled you aside to inspire you, a teacher took some time after class to encourage you, or someone unexpected placed their confidence and trust in you. We remember these moments. Someone else saw your potential and took a chance on you. These moments shape the course of our lives, and in many cases, the other person doesn't even remember it. To them, they weren't doing anything special, but because they made the choice to bet on you, you became something different. You became something more. Maybe they didn't notice it, but you'll never forget it. This describes the enduring impact of effective leadership.

Leadership is a quality of human relationships. The only thing you need is a willing follower. Followers have a choice, and so do you. Leaders choose courage when fear tells them to stop. Leaders choose confidence to move forward even when they lack certainty of the path. Despite the fallibility of our nature, leaders place their faith and trust in people. Leadership isn't a function of position or authority; it is a deliberate choice. If you are willing to choose the people, you can lead and win in today's modern VUCA reality.

By the very nature of the VUCA reality, the only constant in any military unit or civilian organization is the people. That is why leaders provide the decisive edge. Leadership means being the example to connect and inspire others under ordinary conditions so you can achieve and win under extraordinary circumstances. Management - the expedient, "cozy-dog" move - can't do this. Leadership - the spendthrift moral act - can. Leaders make better people, and in doing so, the most capable team for any situation. That's how you win. Given their experience, this is the unique value military leaders offer civilian society when they become veterans.

Unfortunately, veterans are a disappearing segment of our population. The simple fact is there just aren't enough veterans to bring the vital lessons of leadership from the military back to civilian society in any measurable or sustainable way. Because fewer people are connected to the military service, the true value of this leadership experience is often lost or misunderstood. Much to the detriment of our nation, the gap between society and those individuals sworn to protect it continues to widen. The next two chapters explain why this gap exists and what makes the leadership development experience in the military different from nonmilitary approaches. In later chapters, we introduce the ADAPT Framework to bridge the gap between military leadership and nonmilitary applications in the VUCA reality. "ADAPT" is an acronym for leader behaviors from the military that breaks down like this:

- **Align** Values and Purpose to Inspire Performance
- **Develop** a Culture of Camaraderie
- **Apply** the Hierarchy of Organizational Agility
- **Process** Optimization for Coordinated Action and Decentralized Execution
- **Transform** Leader Engagement through the Coach, Teach, and Mentor Methodology

This model takes the tested and proven practices, doctrine, and lessons learned from the military to help aspiring leaders in nonmilitary organizations lead, achieve, and win in the modern VUCA reality. Never before have the thousands of pages of military doctrine been distilled to create a new and original framework for understanding the art of leading others in nonmilitary applications. This book translates the best of military leadership for civilian purposes, bringing both worlds closer together.

The VUCA world is here to stay. It's time to acknowledge what we once characterized as an emergency situation is just a part of the new normal. This is the modern world we live in. Our challenge has less to do with how prepared we are for the next crisis as it is about how we prepare leaders to step up and thrive through any crisis.

I understand the rationale behind why we use business metrics to assess leadership effectiveness. Numbers are predictable. People are not. It is easy to justify actions and decisions based on the bottom line. We say it's not personal. It's just business. Unfortunately, a business management approach that relies on systems, consistency, and process doesn't have the *resilience, agility*, or *dependability* to survive the modern crisis. Where business models fail, people endure. This is why betting on your people is the only practical choice.

It's ironic that leadership is so often characterized as a "soft" skill. For anyone who has experienced one of these leadership moments, there is nothing soft about it. When we are at our worst is when we need leaders to step up and be at their best. When the outcome has no guarantees or promises, that is when people need leadership the most. Finding the courage to choose the spendthrift moral act instead of hitting the easy button is hard - really hard. Leadership - the kind that rises to the challenge of a defining moment - is not a privilege. It's a burden.

I felt this burden on the day JC and Andre died. In hindsight, nothing I did that day was special, but it remains one of the hardest days of my life. Standing to face our soldiers and what transpired over the next twelve hours was a surreal experience. I didn't get to choose the leadership moment. It chose me. That's the point. Whether it's a market crash, coronavirus, terrorist attacks, a hurricane, or losing two of your soldiers in Afghanistan, there is no way to predict how the challenge - your leadership moment - might unfold, but when it comes to assessing a leader's effectiveness, that is the only moment that counts. If you are ready for this challenge, then let's talk about how you might learn from the military experience to inspire others with the confidence, competence, and commitment to win in today's modern VUCA reality.

2 | THE DISAPPEARANCE OF THE VETERAN IN MODERN SOCIETY

The credit belongs to the man who is actually in the arena, whose face is marred by dust and sweat and blood; who strives valiantly; who errs, who comes short again and again, because there is no effort without error and shortcoming; but who does actually strive to do the deeds; who knows great enthusiasms, the great devotions; who spends himself in a worthy cause; who at the best knows in the end the triumph of high achievement, and who at the worst, if he fails, at least fails while daring greatly, so that his place shall never be with those cold and timid souls who neither know victory nor defeat.

- *Theodore Roosevelt*

Let's begin by exploring the value of military service beyond the battlefield. In primitive cultures, the warrior experience was a rite of passage to identify the most capable leaders. It was the crucible to forge the character and wisdom of the wise elders, chieftains, and statesmen who served and led the social order. In the modern era, the titles have changed from warrior to soldier, sailor, airmen, or marine, but their contribution to the healthy function of society has not. Today's military leaders return from the battlefield and become veteran leaders in our communities, at our places of work, and in our public offices. Unfortunately, the veteran leader has become an endangered segment of our society.

The average citizen has become increasingly detached from the military experience. In 2020, there were almost 2.2 million active duty, reserve, and guard component service members in a nation of nearly 330 million people.[5] Compare that number to the nearly 12 million service members in 1945 for a nation of only 140 million people.[6] Here in the United States, our military was more than five times the size for about one-third the population. As the population increased over the years, participation in the armed forces has decreased.

This trend has obvious consequences to veteran participation in the labor force. In 1985, one out of every four men in the workforce between the ages of 30 and 44 had served in the military.[7] By 2019, the number of veterans (both men and women) in the workforce dropped to only one in every fifteen employees.[8] Because a majority of today's veteran population comes from the Vietnam Era, we can expect veteran participation in the labor force to decrease substantially as these men and women enter later stages of life.

When we eliminated the draft in 1973, military service became a voluntary choice instead of a social obligation, and society absorbed some unintended consequences. A smaller percentage of our elected officials have had military experience. During the 1970s, over 70 percent of elected representatives and more than 80 percent of senators were veterans, but by 2017, that number dropped to barely 20 percent for both Houses of Congress.[9] As the number of veteran politicians decreased, so too has the approval ratings of our elected officials to the lowest levels in recorded history.[10] Is this a coincidence or a sign of a deeper correlation?

The lack of veterans also impacted leadership across the economic sector. At the end of the Second World War, nearly 50 percent of new small businesses - a significant segment of the U.S. economy - were created by veterans, but only 5 percent of veterans in the post-9/11 era started their own business.[11] In the 1980s, 60 percent of CEOs had military experience compared to less than 8 percent of CEOs in 2012.[12] Given the preponderance of corporate malfeasance since the turn of the century, it is worth noting that nonveterans are 60 percent more likely to preside over ethical and legal transgressions than their veteran counterparts.[13] Because the warrior archetype and veteran leadership play a role in the healthy function of society, their marginalization comes with some unfortunate consequences.

These consequences are more pronounced once you step inside the front door of a corporate office. In 2016, the Millennial Generation became the largest contributor to the American workforce, and it is worth noting that 71 percent of millennials do not feel engaged at work.[14] In his book, *Speed of Trust*, Steven Covey noted that only 45 percent of employees have trust in senior management, only 18 percent of people believe business leaders tell them the truth, and 76 percent of employees over a 12 month period observed illegal or unethical conduct.[15] Employees are so disconnected and unhappy at work that almost 70 percent of them are actively searching for a new job.[16] In terms of the coveted bottom line, millennial turnover is costing the U.S. economy almost $30.5 billion annually.[17]

Let's face it. Across our communities and neighborhoods, we have become a society divided. The once noble melting pot has become increasingly contentious to our fellow citizens based on gender, color, ethnicity, religion, or political affiliation. We debate whether or not the land of the free needs to be surrounded by walls. We honor freedom of expression based on the condition of how you stand - or kneel - before the flag. We've witnessed the storming of our nation's capital for the first time in over two centuries. We distinguish ourselves from the American fabric based on our differences instead of uniting hands based on our shared values, purpose, and vision. We look for the worst in each other, and too often expose the worst in ourselves.

Since the dawn of civilization, the warrior experience has prepared, inspired, and forged individuals with the qualities for leadership responsibility beyond the military. It is not coincidence that the fragmentation of our society is occurring at a rate commensurate with the shrinking presence of veteran leaders across our nation. Disconnection and polarization have defined our state of being. Fewer veterans means fewer leaders forged through the military experience.

We can be better. People want to be inspired. We want to be a part of something bigger than ourselves. We want to be that example, the shining house on a hill - a beacon of hope. We want to be the good guys. In these uncertain times, we need to be the best versions of ourselves. Now more than ever, we are a nation starving for leadership.

3 | WHAT MAKES MILITARY LEADERS DIFFERENT

The ultimate measure of a man is not where he stands in moments of convenience and comfort, but where he stands at times of challenge and controversy.

-   Martin Luther King, Jr.

Since the fall of the Soviet Union in 1991, the scope of known missions for the military has expanded to include anything and everything the national command authority deems vital to the security or interests of our nation. In the post 9/11 era, the mission profile for a single unit could include combat, counterterrorism, counterinsurgency, support of civilian authorities, peacekeeping, training host nation military forces, and institutional training or support. When the expectation of the nation is to win under any condition, leaders have no choice but to focus on the capacity and capability of their people to accomplish any mission. As a consequence of this strategic reality, military leaders bear the responsibility to coach, teach, and mentor service members to perform at the upper limit of their potential.

The military's focus on people provides a competitive edge, and there are two basic but distinct qualities differentiating military leaders from their nonmilitary counterparts. First, leader identity takes precedence over a professional or functional identity, which are the job titles derived from how the commercial sector structures its workforce. Regardless of the operating specialty, the military shapes a service member's intention to step up and lead regardless of the situation. Second, all military leaders accept personal responsibility for the preparation of tomorrow's leaders through coaching, teaching, and mentoring. Every instance in training or combat is a teachable moment. Regardless of the circumstances, the people are always the mission.

Leader Identity vs. Functional Identity

Leadership development begins the moment a new recruit enters the military. This process intends to develop "an identity that's embedded in their persona, so that in any circumstance, they're going to emerge as leaders."[18] A strong leader identity is defined by the qualities of confidence, competence, and commitment. Let's explore what that means for you.

Confidence is believing that winning is possible. Winning is not about competition or ego, but about overcoming challenges to emerge as a team in a better place on the other side. Regardless of the situation, confident leaders believe in a positive vision and outcome, which inspires hope in otherwise desperate situations. That hope becomes a source of shared energy. It allows people to set their differences aside, join efforts, and make things happen. **Competence** combines a leader's ability and understanding of the situation with their skills in communication and analysis to create opportunities for decisive action. As a fundamental need to connect with others, leadership requires a **commitment** to honor all relationships between the leader and their team by developing trust and showing empathy over time. This doesn't happen overnight.

These qualities are mutually supportive and independently, cannot stand on their own. The confident leader who lacks competence and commitment is foolhardy. The toxic leader is one who is confident and competent but has no commitment to the people. The competent leader without confidence will not have the courage to act. The committed leader who lacks confidence and competence seeks acceptance and likability over respect. **A leader who lacks all three - confidence, competence, and commitment - shies away from responsibility, takes credit for the work of others, and manipulates others for selfish reasons.** You may have seen one or more examples of managers like this, but if not, does this sound like the kind of person you would want to follow?

On the flip side, leaders with all three have the ability and desire to develop meaningful, professional relationships where they place confidence in the competence of each individual on the team. The synergy from these three qualities defines a leader identity to win in the VUCA reality.

A service member's functional identity - as defined by military operating specialty or occupation - is subordinate to their leader identity. Leadership - performance and potential - is the determining factor in evaluations, promotions, and career opportunities. Each military rank comes with a set of clear expectations to perform at a level beyond their education or experience, facilitating growth in the confidence, competence, and commitment of their leader identity. Leaders are expected to be uncomfortable as they grow into their position. Once they've mastered that position, they are assigned to another, and the cycle repeats itself. Performance is important, but the military bets on potential.

Aggressive career management is how the military develops leaders with the innate skill of being comfortable in unfamiliar or uncomfortable situations. Imagine placing a pilot with no prior training or appropriate credentials as the director of human resources for an organization of up to 1,000 people. Consider the possibility of holding an infantry officer, affectionately referred to as a knuckle dragger, with no business or accounting experience in charge of managing a multimillion dollar budget. Assignments into unfamiliar roles with a tremendous amount of responsibility with little or no prior training or experience occur on a routine basis in the military. The leader's responsibility is to figure it out, and - despite their lack of expertise - to provide the necessary purpose, direction, and motivation to be successful. Some may see this as trial by fire, but good leaders learn quickly that it's not about them or the specific task. It's about their team. The team already has the necessary knowledge and expertise. Their job is to lead.

As soon as these leaders get just enough experience to be competent, the military moves them to a different position, organization, or installation. It is not uncommon for a leader to have a myriad of functional experiences in 12 to 36 month intervals spanning the duration of a 20 year career. This provides leaders growth opportunities to gain competence, build confidence, and forge commitments with new people and is integral to the holistic development of their leader identity. By shifting to a new role or new organization every two years, leaders are able to fine-tune their leadership skills. They get exposed to different leaders and subordinates with unique styles, approaches, and personalities. Throughout the military journey, each subsequent position increases in size and scope: more people, more responsibilities, and more challenges. When you constantly thrust leaders into uncomfortable situations, they develop a certain confidence - an edge - to operate and succeed in any environment.

By contrast, civilian professionals identify based on functional expertise - engineer, doctor, lawyer, electrician, etc. Leadership is secondary to functional expertise for career progression. Competence is measured by productivity, efficiency, and profitability. Engineers with the highest quality of work become engineering managers. The most competent surgeons become chiefs of medicine.

The people with the best sales numbers become regional sales managers. Promotions are based largely on past performance within a particular specialty.

New managers, who are competent in their trade, are now in charge of managing and leading teams. Now they're not just responsible for their specialty, but they're also dealing with people - the good, bad, and the ugly. The opportunity to develop the confidence to provide direction, guidance, and motivation in uncomfortable situations doesn't begin until they are expected to lead. Functional competence does not predict leadership potential, and consequently, many new managers simply lack the interpersonal skills to succeed.

A quick sidebar and something to consider, the fourth industrial revolution is upon us.[19] Smart technologies, automation, and machine to machine learning are evolving manufacturing and industrial practices. What will the employment landscape look like 5 to 10 years from now? How will the labor force evolve? We already see the ripple effects from emerging technology. Universities educate students in functional specialties, yet many students struggle to find jobs after graduation. In many cases, those functions and specialties have been consumed by new innovations.

The World Economic Forum predicts a shift in the educational system from a monodisciplinary approach to one that is interdisciplinary.[20] Graduates will be generalists with a specialization, but at the crux, they will be problem solvers and critical thinkers. In other words, the approach for secondary education in the civilian world will gravitate toward the military's capabilities-based approach to develop leaders who can solve complex problems and find a way to succeed in any situation.

When individuals with a strong leader identity are placed in charge of an organization or team, the people are valued as assets. They have to be. They have the functional expertise. If you want to see whether an organization views its people as assets or liabilities, watch what happens during a crisis. When the people define the organization, leaders bear the burdens and make the necessary sacrifices to motivate the team. They recognize that the people are the source of productive output. Therefore, the leaders muster the personal energy to infuse optimism to inspire the team. They place as much faith in the team as they expect the team to place in them. When the chips are down, leaders expose themselves to the dangers by standing in front of their formation. In times of crisis when resources become scarce, leaders eat last.

A great demonstration of this is through the example of Gravity Payments, a credit card processing company for 20,000 small businesses.[21] During the 2020 pandemic, the company was losing $1.5 million a month. They had reached the point where they had about 90 days before going out of business. Dan Price, the company's CEO, confronted his team of 200 employees with brutal honesty and vulnerability regarding what the company was facing. He looked to his people. He placed his faith in the team. To his surprise, the team offered a solution in lieu of layoffs. They volunteered nearly half a million dollars from their salaries. Some employees even offered their total paycheck. Their commitment to the company earned just enough time to bounce back. By late summer, Dan paid back the employees. Some even got a pay raise!

The success of Gravity Payments during this crisis was made possible because Dan had already demonstrated his commitment to the people. Five years earlier, Dan took a pay cut to institute a $70K minimum salary for his employees. He made the sacrifice. He paid it forward and chose to eat last. Because he placed his confidence and commitment in the people, the people trusted his leadership and were committed to the organization. This example is newsworthy because too many executives choose to eat first and take their share at the expense of the people.[22] Executives get bonuses while employees get pink slips. Instead of profits, Dan chose the people, and it made all the difference. When money is the glue that keeps an organization together, it will fall apart when the money disappears. Money comes and goes. People endure. Gravity Payments succeeded because Dan chose the spendthrift moral act.

Expanding Leadership Growth as Coach, Teacher, and Mentor

As it stands today, senior executives of companies are not typically the primary coaches, teachers, and mentors for their organization. In fact, many executives don't ever coach, teach, *or* mentor. According to the 2016 SHRM/Globoforce Employee Recognition Survey, only 56 percent of managers coach their employees despite the fact 66 percent of HR professionals believe coaching is a vital factor in performance management.[23] A staggering 93 percent of HR professionals believe managers lack the coaching skills essential to be effective leaders.[24] Other research shows that, "39 percent of new managers with fewer than three years on the job reported receiving any leadership training, just 34 percent received any mentoring, and a mere 31 percent received coaching."[25] At no fault of their own, civilian managers don't have the same preparation as their military counterparts to lead and inspire in the modern VUCA reality.

The nature of the VUCA environment requires individuals at all levels to elevate their game. As a military leader, you might be the person in charge, but that doesn't mean you are the smartest or most capable person in the room. The leader's job is to inspire everyone on the team to give their best performance. This is done through a combination of **self-awareness** (to understand their strengths) and **self-actualization** (to discover their potential). Leaders engage with compassion and an open mind to discover and expand the capacity and capability of the team.

We've talked about the importance of leader identity. Drawing parallels from the military, the next step in your growth as a leader is learning to integrate coaching, teaching, and mentoring into your leadership style and interpersonal engagement. This is the practical application of the spendthrift moral act. We will introduce the leader roles as the coach, teacher, and mentor (CTM) here and discuss how to apply these roles later through the CTM Methodology.

Coach - Volunteer recruits must be inspired in order to persevere and endure the burden and sacrifice of military service. Service members have to want to be there, which is no different than what is required in today's civilian workforce. This is where coaching plays a key role. By definition, a coaching relationship is a partnership that helps an individual identify goals and strategies to achieve them. This partnership is built on trust, empathy, and accountability. Coaches help individuals see who they are and where they fit in the bigger picture of the organization. This process aligns an individual's values and purpose with the shared values and sense of purpose for the organization.

Teach - As the teacher, military leaders treat training events as experiential learning opportunities for leadership growth and professional development. Training exercises are often rigged for the unit to fail. They include unforeseen contingencies designed to test the upper limits of a unit's capacity and capability. By revealing vulnerabilities, the leader can take action to mitigate risk and/or develop a strategy for improvement. Where a knowledge gap exists, education is provided. Where junior leaders lack experience or confidence, they provide guidance. Where there are developmental opportunities, leaders provide constructive feedback.

Military training conditions leaders to be comfortable in remarkably uncomfortable situations. The military believes that if the training conditions are more difficult than what might be expected in combat, that leader will have the confidence and composure to make sound decisions, provide direction, and motivate their unit when lives are really on the line. Frequency and repetition provide an iterative process to apply lessons learned. In a nonmilitary context, David Kelley, CEO and founder of IDEO - a global design and innovation company, echoes this through his approach to "Fail fast. Succeed sooner."[26] Through these experiential learning opportunities, leaders develop effective problem solving habits to navigate the VUCA environment. As the teacher, leaders challenge employees to work at the limit of their capability, encourage professional development, and guide learning through exposure to problems they don't yet know how to solve.

Mentor - Mentor relationships represent a decisive advantage of the leadership development experience in the military. In a culture that values selfless service and a commitment to something greater than yourself, having someone recognize you as a mentor is one of the most rewarding forms of personal validation as a military leader. This is perhaps the biggest missing piece from the leadership puzzle in today's society. It's also the most difficult to implement because you cannot simply assign a mentor. Young leaders must find their own mentor - someone they respect and whose footsteps they are inclined to follow.

Gone are the days of apprenticeships. The modern protégé learns from a mentor. Mentorship spans both personal and professional topics alike. Many mentor relationships in the military evolve into lifelong friendships. Both as a mentor and mentee, these relationships have been the most transformative for my own personal and professional growth. The people you mentor become the living legacy for a military career, and they can define your legacy regardless of your profession.

Because the military is an all-volunteer force, leaders must inspire loyalty and commitment from individuals and their families for continued military service. Your organization can do the same through developing personal connections as the foundation for professional relationships. Without this foundation of trust, belonging, and intrinsic motivation, people eventually and inevitably stop volunteering. Coaching, teaching, and mentoring are essential job requirements for today's leader - military or otherwise. Leaders who act as the coach, teacher, and mentor embody the inherent belief that better individuals make a more capable team. The military leader bets on their people, and that is what makes all the difference.

4 | HOW AND WHY MILITARY LEADERSHIP WORKS IN THE VUCA REALITY

A leader is best when people barely know he exists, when his work is done, his aim fulfilled, they will say: we did it ourselves.

- Lao Tzu

We discussed what makes military leadership different, and now, we will show how and why it works in the VUCA reality. The remainder of this book teaches you how to apply the same approach to your organization or place of business. Our goal is to inspire confidence, instill competence, and build commitment by forging your leader identity, so you are prepared to handle whatever challenges your organization might endure in today's uncertain world.

We took the army's model of leadership and filtered it through the science of emotional intelligence. The net result is a comparative analysis between the foundation of leadership philosophy in the military and the best practices in behavioral science for optimizing individual contributions to high performance teams. This recalibration of military doctrine for practical, nonmilitary applications validates the universal benefit of best practices from the military for any organization.

We chose emotional intelligence as the standard for this comparison because of its evidence-based impact on high performance outcomes. "Studies have found that high emotional intelligence in organizations is associated with increased productivity, higher engagement levels, lower turnover and absenteeism rates, and increased market share."[27] Other research shows that leaders who score high in emotional intelligence are seven times more likely to have high performance outcomes.[28] If you type "emotional intelligence" into your search engine, your browser returns millions of results including articles, programs, and other tools intended to develop these traits deemed essential to achieve higher levels of performance. *Emotional intelligence is not required to manage, but it is essential if you intend to lead - and lead effectively.*

The importance of emotional intelligence in today's military is tied to the end of the Cold War. The fall of the Soviet Union created a new strategic reality that required emotionally intelligent leaders. The national defense strategy shifted from a threat centric approach to a capabilities centric approach. At the same time, the absence of an existential threat placed downward pressure on the defense budget. The mission profile for the military increased while the resources for achieving those missions decreased. The institutional mindset throughout the 1990s was to "do more with less." By the simple law of supply and demand, the value of each volunteer wearing the uniform went up because there were fewer service members being asked to take on more responsibilities.

The culture in military units became an area of concern and continues to be a high priority today. Despite the increasing workload, leaders had to create organizational climates where people wanted to be there. Units with positive command climates (leaders with high levels of emotional intelligence) perform better, do more, and retain the most capable service members with the highest potential. Conversely, toxic leaders with poor command climates were dysfunctional, often unethical, and were seemingly pushing many high performers out of the service. More than ever, the military needed leaders with a high competency in the practice of emotional intelligence.

To prove this point, let's compare the traits of emotional intelligence to the attributes and competencies from the Army Leadership Requirements Model. Emotional Intelligence erupted in the 1990s as the result of a collaboration between three generational disruptors within the fields of psychology, organizational behavior, and education. In their seminal work, *Primal Leadership: Realizing the Power of Emotional Intelligence*, Dan Goleman, Richard Boyatzis, and Annie McKee began a movement for understanding how the science of emotions impacted business performance. By comparison, the Army Leadership Requirements Model provides a standard of leadership behavior based on the qualities of BE (Character and Presence), KNOW (Intellect), and DO (Leads, Develops, and Achieves).[29] We sifted through army doctrine in Figures I through 4 to illustrate how the traits for emotional intelligence align with specific attributes and competencies from the Army Leadership Requirements Model.[30]

EMOTIONAL INTELLIGENCE COMPETENCY: SELF-AWARENESS

EMOTIONAL INTELLIGENCE TRAITS		ARMY LEADERSHIP MODEL ATTRIBUTES AND COMPETENCIES	
Emotional Self-Awareness	The ability to read and understand your emotions as well as recognize their impact on work performance, relationships, and the like	Interpersonal Tact	Understanding the character, reactions, and motives of oneself and others[31]
Accurate Self-Assessment	A realistic evaluation of your strengths and weaknesses	Prepares Self	Self-awareness enables leaders to recognize their strengths and weaknesses across a range of conditions and progressively employ strengths to correct weaknesses[32]
Self-Confidence	A strong and positive sense of self-worth	Confidence	Projective self-confidence and certainty in the unit's ability to accomplish the mission, able to retain composure and demonstrate calm through steady control over emotion[33]

Figure 1. Comparison between Emotional Intelligence and the Army Leadership Requirements Model for the Competency of Self-Awareness

EMOTIONAL INTELLIGENCE COMPETENCY: SELF-MANAGEMENT

EMOTIONAL INTELLIGENCE TRAITS		ARMY LEADERSHIP MODEL ATTRIBUTES AND COMPETENCIES	
Self-Control	The ability to keep disruptive emotions and impulses under control	Discipline	The ability to control one's own behavior[34]
		Interpersonal Tact	Emotional self-control, balance, and stability enable leaders to make sound, ethical decisions[35]
Trustworthiness	A consistent display of honesty and integrity	Humility	A person of high integrity, honesty, and character embodies the qualities of humility[36]
Conscientiousness	The ability to manage yourself and your responsibilities	Leads by Example	Sets the example by modeling expected standards of duty performance, personal appearance, military and professional bearing, physical fitness, and ethics[37]
Adaptability	Skill at adjusting to changing situations and overcoming obstacles	Mental Agility	Anticipating or adapting to uncertain or changing situations; thinking through outcomes when current decisions or actions are not producing desired effects[38]
Achievement Orientation	The drive to meet an internal standard of excellence	Leads by Example	Performs duty with discipline and to standard, while striving for excellence[39]
Initiative	A readiness to seize opportunities	Mental Agility	A leader's mental agility to quickly isolate a problem and identify solutions facilitates seizing initiative and adapting effectively[40]

Figure 2. Comparison between Emotional Intelligence and the Army Leadership Requirements Model for the Competency of Self-Monitoring

EMOTIONAL INTELLIGENCE COMPETENCY: SOCIAL AWARENESS

EMOTIONAL INTELLIGENCE TRAITS		ARMY LEADERSHIP MODEL ATTRIBUTES AND COMPETENCIES	
Empathy	Skill at sensing other people's emotions, understanding their perspective, and taking an active interest in their concerns	Empathy	Army leaders show empathy when they genuinely relate to another person's situation, motives, or feelings[41]
Organizational Awareness	The ability to read the currents of organizational life, build decision networks, and navigate politics	Extends Influence Beyond the Chain of Command	Assesses situations, missions, and assignments to determine the parties involved in decision making, decision support, and possible interference or resistance[42]
Service Orientation	The ability to recognize and meet customers' needs	Warrior Ethos/ Service Ethos	A soldier's selfless commitment to the Nation, mission, unit, and fellow soldiers[43]

Figure 3. Comparison between Emotional Intelligence and the Army Leadership Requirements Model for the Competency of Social Awareness

EMOTIONAL INTELLIGENCE COMPETENCY: SOCIAL SKILL		
EMOTIONAL INTELLIGENCE TRAITS		**ARMY LEADERSHIP MODEL ATTRIBUTES AND COMPETENCIES**
Visionary Leadership	The ability to take charge and inspire with a compelling vision	Leads Others	Leaders motivate, inspire, and influence others to take initiative, work toward a common purpose, accomplish critical tasks, and achieve organizational objectives. Influence focuses on compelling others to go beyond their individual interests and to work for the common good[44]
Influence	The ability to wield a range of persuasive tactics	Leads Others	Army leaders employ various methods of direct influence based on audience, intent, and context of the situation[45]
Developing Others	The propensity to bolster the abilities others through feedback and guidance	Develops Others	Assesses development need of others; counsels, coaches, and mentors; facilitates ongoing development[46]
Communication	Skill at listening and at sending clear, convincing, and well-tuned messages	Communicates	Leaders communicate effectively by clearly expressing ideas and actively listening to others[47]
Change Catalyst	Proficiency in initiating new ideas and leading people in new directions	Innovation	Innovation describes the ability to introduce or implement something new[48]
Conflict Management	The ability to deescalate disagreements and orchestrate resolutions	Creates a Positive Environment/ Fosters Esprit de Corps	Identify and resolve conflict before it affects personal and organizational functioning, good order and discipline, and cohesion[49]
Building Bonds	Proficiency at cultivating and maintaining a web of relationships	Builds Trust	Fosters positive relationships with others[50]
Teamwork and Collaboration	Competence at promoting cooperation and building teams	Creates a Positive Environment/ Fosters Esprit de Corps	Fosters teamwork, cohesion, cooperation, loyalty and esprit de corps[51]

Figure 4. Comparison between Emotional Intelligence and the Army Leadership Requirements Model for the Competency of Social Skill

The similarities are uncanny. Each of the traits associated with emotional intelligence is accounted for in at least one of the attributes or competencies in the Army Leadership Requirements Model. In some cases, it is almost word for word. From this comparison, we can conclude the Army Leadership Requirements Model is an application of the proven science of emotional intelligence. This is important, because *every* leadership practice in the army originates from this model. **Because it is grounded in the science of emotional intelligence, the army's model and the techniques that spring from it are universally applicable to military and nonmilitary organizations alike.**

The level of exposure to the science through this model is where military leaders currently enjoy an advantage over their civilian counterparts. Because the military profession focuses on leader identity, these proven qualities for successful leadership provide the foundation for education, training, assessment, and promotion through the *entire* lifecycle of a service member's career. There is an acknowledgement that leadership is a priority and clarity in what the military expects from its leaders. Leaders from within the organization are responsible for providing the needed training and development for their teams, which reinforces their contributions to the broader culture of the organization. By the time an officer reaches a position of command for up to 1,000 soldiers, they've had two decades of instruction, experience, evaluation, and feedback in the science of emotional intelligence. Given the depth and circumstances of this application, they are perhaps the most proficient practitioners of emotional intelligence in modern society.

A high degree of emotional intelligence is what enables military leaders to operate effectively outside their specific functional area of training. Leaders don't need to be the source of specialized knowledge or technical expertise, but they do need to build trust and confidence with those who are. They expand the capability and capacity of the organization by including and empowering subordinates to optimize decisions, solutions, and results. This is what makes the military leader so effective in the VUCA environment.

The alignment between leadership in the military and the science of emotional intelligence reveals an opportunity that can benefit leaders in any organization.

We know the military experience develops confident and competent leaders who are willing to wade into remarkably uncomfortable situations. We also know that nonmilitary organizations will continue to face uncomfortable challenges. We can't generate more veterans to integrate these leadership lessons organically into society the way we did during the last century. The civil-military gap will continue to widen as the percentage of veterans actively participating in the workforce continues to decline. We can't change the trending demographics or environment, but we can bridge the gap by offering the best practices of military leadership and operations under VUCA conditions for nonmilitary applications.

The ADAPT Framework is the bridge between military and civilian leadership. As shown in Figure 5 below, the ADAPT Framework applies the science of psychology and organizational behavior to underscore what works in the military and how those best practices might apply to you. It empowers leaders to focus on any organization's most valuable asset - the people - to unleash individual potential to achieve beyond the limits of what is considered possible. The ADAPT Framework is how we close the gap of leadership across our society.

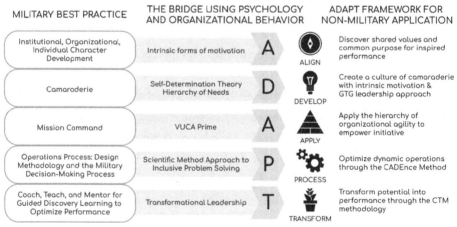

Figure 5. The ADAPT Framework bridges military best practices and business applications.

In the following chapters, we explore each of the five elements of the ADAPT Framework. This model equips leaders with the tools to put the people first. This framework provides an approach to develop and empower leaders across the organization to thrive and win in the modern VUCA reality.

5 | ALIGN VALUES AND PURPOSE TO INSPIRE PERFORMANCE

The two most important days in your life are the day you are born and the day you find out why.

- Mark Twain

The ADAPT Framework is built upon a foundation of **character** - a deeper analysis of our personal values and purpose. If you want to understand what motivates others, start by understanding what motivates you. Know *your* values and *your* purpose. These are the intrinsic qualities that shape and direct who you are and what activities you find meaningful. Your values and purpose are the guideposts for the choices you make personally and professionally.

We want to be inspired. We want to experience passion. We innately want to perform at our best. According to Maslow's Hierarchy of Needs, self-actualization, achieving one's fullest potential, is the pinnacle of healthy psychological development. At this point fulfillment, passion, and joy come together. *We feel alive.* We spend our lives striving to reach this point, and our values and purpose show us how to get there.

Personal values and purpose define your character. Values reveal WHO you are. They are traits and qualities enduring beyond professional titles or other conventional labels to describe your uniqueness as an individual. Titles, roles, and salaries are given to you by someone else. They can also be taken away. Values are embedded in your DNA. They represent your inner compass orienting you to your true North. Purpose describes WHY you are here. Activities aligned to your purpose run on intrinsic forms of motivation - the most effective and sustainable form of personal drive and energy. You feel good when you do things that align with your purpose. Together, these two qualities provide the direction and energy to reach your full potential.

Organizations are also living entities. Like people, they have a set of values and a purpose that direct action and provide the motivation to realize their full potential. Values and purpose represent the essence of an organization. They breathe life into the otherwise inanimate functions, processes, and exchanges that define the business environment. Just as many people go through life without understanding their WHO or WHY, many organizations fail to recognize their shared values and greater purpose to society. This is not to say organizations don't have values or some form of a mission statement, but too often, these are nothing more than framed clichés on an office wall, a footnote on the corporate website, or an entry in their annual earnings report. They are nothing more than window dressings on an empty house. If an organization doesn't have a strong core of values and purpose, they lack the durability and fortitude to survive in today's VUCA environment.

Let's look at an example. In 2000, Communication, Respect, Integrity, and Excellence were the corporate values that Enron, an energy trader and supplier corporation, listed in their annual report.[52] These words are attractive to corporate investors, but they held no meaning to the people in the company. This conclusion is based on the fact that Enron was the architect of one of the largest scandals of corruption and unethical accounting practices in U.S. history. Their actions resulted in the dissolution of Arthur Andersen, one of the top accounting firms in the nation at the time. Based on what the company actually did, you could argue that making money provided the direction and motivation for their behavior.

Enron published a set of words they thought outside investors wanted to see, but at their core, their leadership was extremely self-interested. Enron's leadership boasted that they were the smartest guys in the room.[53] They may have been the smartest, but they certainly weren't the most ethical. When the money got scarce, illicit behavior was never out of the question. You might even say it was the preferred course of action. Without a strong character grounded in values and purpose, an organization crumbles under the pressure of a crisis.

In the VUCA environment, information changes and circumstances evolve, but everyone's commitment to shared values and a common purpose provides clarity - a compass - through the fog of ambiguity. Had just one of Enron's executives been true to their values, they might have intervened well before indictments became inevitable. This is why the military starts with character and builds a culture valuing trust and ethics. In critical situations, they rely on leaders at all levels to make ethical decisions and behave in a manner in keeping with the values of the organization.

Here are some of the benefits of grounding an organization in a shared set of values with a common purpose:

Character endures. Values don't change with professional titles, rank, or position. They provide the common denominator connecting leaders performing different roles, executing different missions, and operating in different locations. Shared values reveal the authentic identity of the organization. In the military, character binds together the diverse population of men and women who volunteer to wear the uniform.

Values and purpose fuel our intrinsic drive. We feel the most passionate and committed to activities aligned with our values and purpose. When we accomplish purpose driven activities, we feel inspired to venture beyond what we thought was possible. This motivation is unique to you and is independent of your environment. In the words of the 19th-century philosopher Frederick Nietzsche, "A person who has a WHY can suffer any HOW."

Values instill calm. In the VUCA environment, values provide the one known factor that can instill a sense of calm. Regardless of the crisis or calamity, character provides a reliable constant. Leaders who are grounded in values and purpose are not distracted by a false sense of urgency, appearances, or external validation. They remain steady through the chaos of overwhelming situations.

Character inspires trust. Rank and title compel compliance, but character instills trust. You cannot compel a person to trust you. It is something they must do willingly. This requires courage to be seen outside the cover and concealment of your role, position, or title. It requires vulnerability to reveal the underlying truth of one's character. When a leader exposes their character - the WHO and the WHY, they are able to connect authentically with others. From a core of shared values and common purpose, members of a team identify as one.

Character empowers. Success in the VUCA environment requires empowered leaders who trust in themselves to make calculated decisions and create opportunities. The army calls this mission command (a concept we will discuss later in greater detail). Leaders trust that subordinates who share common values and purpose can interpret circumstances and derive solutions consistent with the shared identity of the organization. This builds faith in the potential of leaders across the team to make the right decisions and take the appropriate actions in any situation.

When the VUCA reality introduces a new crisis, organizations with a strong character based on shared values and a common purpose close ranks, become stronger, and harness the intrinsic drive, talent, and potential from its members to persevere and succeed.

Creating a character-based organization unleashes the power and potential of intrinsic forms of motivation. A crisis can deprive an organization of resources and limit options. The lack of external incentives elevates the importance of an individual's will and determination to see the organization succeed. If the situation is bad enough, that might be all you've got. The good news is that "no single phenomenon reflects the positive potential of human nature as much as intrinsic motivation."[54] **Intrinsic motivation** is where the behavior itself provides its own reward. At some point, there is a limit to external incentives, but there is no limit to the motivation and drive from within. When people are motivated intrinsically, they see how the objectives of the organization align to their own objectives for personal growth and fulfillment. Intrinsically motivated behaviors inspire people to be their most creative, positive, and committed - qualities essential for navigating a complex and evolving crisis.[55] Your challenge is to harness this power and unlock its potential.

It starts with self-awareness. Understanding values and purpose are the keys to accessing intrinsically motivated behaviors. Once you know your own values and purpose, find others with similar attributes. They don't need to be identical. They only need to align. When you create an organization where individuals and teams are aligned to a shared set of values and a common purpose, you harness the intrinsic motivation on an individual level to achieve and win on an organizational level. The military gets this. This character identity connects with individuals on a deeper level. It inspires the highest effort and active participation in an all-volunteer force despite the dangerous nature of the job. Service members continue volunteering because they believe they are part of something special.

With a strong foundation of character, the people of an organization don't shy away from a challenge. They welcome it. They see adversity as an opportunity to achieve and even surpass their collective potential. The harder the challenge, the larger the stakes, the more desirable the opportunity. This describes the state of motivation for members of high performing military units. They want to be the first to deploy to show the world what they can do. They have an infectious optimism, commitment, and belief that they will find a way to win, and they relish the chance to prove it. Members of these units strive to do their best because the team is counting on them, and in the process, they achieve self-actualization. With individuals and teams performing at the upper limit of their potential, the organization overcomes obstacles to succeed in its mission. Your investment of time and compassion for your people will pay substantial returns. Your people will find ways to take your organization to the next level, much like the Gravity Payments example. This is the power of creating an organization based on the alignment of shared values and a common purpose.

Character Alignment Methodology

All businesses exist to make money. There's nothing wrong with that, but there is a difference between making money and generating true wealth. An impassioned workforce provides the intrinsic energy for your organization to rise to any challenge - especially those in the modern VUCA reality. Money alone can't do that. Character gives you the potential for something more. For the organization, its people, and the communities it serves, a strong organizational character - like a well-rooted tree - might bend and twist during a storm, but it rarely breaks. A shared character that defines the organization is possible when we align individual values and purpose with the values and mission of the organization. If character is rooted in the foundation of your organization, you can persevere and overcome the most difficult challenge in the modern VUCA reality.

From a character perspective, quality and consistency at each level of an organization matter. The army describes the relationship between the individual, the team, and the institution using an apple and barrel metaphor.[56] We've all heard the cliché that one "bad apple" can ruin the entire bunch. We've all been around toxic people who suck the life from an organization. We've also felt the discomfort of being around those people who operate in the "grey space" of moral ambiguity. These are the bad apples. They can poison the organization and make "bad barrels." If the store owners don't do their part to clean out the rotten apples, disinfect the barrels, and provide an environment to maintain both, it becomes a "bad store." The army's multidimensional approach focuses on the individual, organization, and the institution to address the quality of the apples, the barrels, and the store where those apples are sold.

Each of these elements define the shared character of your business. Creating a shared character is a function of institutional culture (the store), the leadership climate of the organization (the barrels), and the character traits of each individual (the apples). Given the importance of character in the leadership development strategy, let's examine more closely how the army leverages these mutually supporting dimensions to create shared values and a common purpose. Figure 6 illustrates what an adaptation of the Army Leadership Development Strategy would look like for an organization like yours:

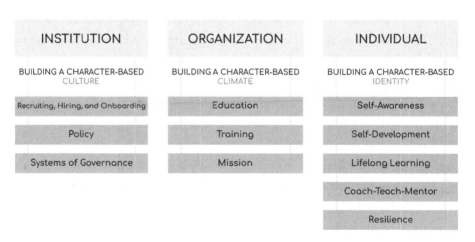

Figure 6. Character Alignment Methodology adapts the Army Leadership Development Strategy with responsibilities for developing shared character traits.[57]

Institution: Build, Sustain, and Reinforce a Character-Based Culture

Culture is an institutional responsibility. By institution, we mean the overall framework, structure, and guidelines for administration and how the organization conducts business. The values and larger purpose provide the core essence that remains constant as people come and go. These traits and qualities must be lived through the actions, behaviors, and decisions of everyone in the organization. They must be respected and, when necessary, dutifully enforced. If individuals behave in a manner inconsistent with the shared values and common purpose, then they must be removed. Like a bad apple, they pose a risk of spoiling the rest of the organization.

The organization establishes an institutional framework for the culture by building, sustaining, and reinforcing the behaviors and activities that align to its values and mission. An organization builds its culture when values and purpose provide the foundation for **recruiting, hiring, and onboarding.** The organization sustains these standards throughout an individual's duration of employment through its **policy** for operations, human resources, training, and professional development. Finally, the organization reinforces the standard through its **systems of governance.** This includes how an organization invests resources to nurture the desired character identity in everything it does, and what actions it takes when those values and purpose are challenged. You see how this institutional approach to character comes full circle. The systems of governance are structured around the premise that the quality of a person's character is more important than the substance of their contribution.

Included in the system is a transparent process to rectify character related transgressions. The military has only one standard: zero tolerance. Any leader who demonstrates unethical behavior is quickly removed from their position of authority. Commanders get relieved. Their reputation or previous performance record doesn't matter. The stakes are too high. All forms of unethical conduct - including harassment and abuse - are handled quickly, decisively, and objectively to maintain the good order and discipline of the unit. The complicit leader who chooses to look the other way is also held accountable and faces the same level of admonishment. These standards are non-negotiable. Conduct inconsistent with the shared values and deeper purpose of the military institution is the mortal sin that will forever condemn the career of any military leader. Bad apples make bad barrels. Bad barrels contaminate other apples and infect the entire store.

How does your organization measure up against this standard? How does your organization measure up against any standard? Standards require consistency. To that end, do the rules change based on a person's position? **How you do anything is how you do everything.** Once you fail to enforce a standard, you've set a new standard. These are difficult questions requiring brutal honesty if you want to align individual attitudes, actions, behaviors, and decisions with the desired character of the organization.

As the essence of the institution, character requires attention, nurturing, and - when necessary - healing. Every organization has a cultural identity - a brand. The question is whether or not that identity is something you want. This is difficult and sometimes uncomfortable work to build, sustain, and reinforce the institutional structure, but if you don't play an active role in building these systems of governance, don't be surprised if your culture is something less than desirable or even toxic.

Organization: Set an Example for a Character-Based Climate

The institution sets the parameters for the culture, but leaders establish the mood - or climate - that reinforces the values and higher purpose of that institution. Leaders set the standard through their actions. Subordinates tend to watch the boss to see what's important and acceptable. In the military, we have a saying that the personality of the unit assumes the personality of the commander. When it comes to character, the leaders must BE the example for the organization - especially when they think no one is watching. The tools that leaders have to create a positive climate and work environment include **education, training,** and how they choose to execute the **mission.**

As the steward for the values and ethics of the organization, commanders take the lead for character-based education and training. Education involves formal and informal opportunities to increase understanding of how to make character-based decisions. Training scenarios often include ethical dilemmas for a deeper conversation about the importance of character-based leadership. Because climate is monitored at multiple echelons of command, surveys are administered routinely throughout a commander's tenure in the unit. Toxic climates result in additional training and feedback, admonishment, or - in extreme cases - removal. Climate is important, because it is easier to fix than culture. Poor climate over time can leave a lasting impact on the reputation and culture of the institution.

The army considers character development an integral part of its mission. We have plenty of tools at our disposal to win on the battlefield. The challenge is to do it honorably. The life and death consequences of military action require adherence to an impeccable standard of character. That standard is interwoven into military operations. Service members have to believe in the cause (purpose) and the means by which they achieve that cause (consistent with the institutional values). This means doing things the right way. Absent this standard, our moral fabric begins to tear from the extreme duress of the combat experience. The subsequent ramifications pose a dire risk to the stability of the service member, the unit, and the entire military institution.

How you do things as a leader matters. The immediate stakes may not be life or death, but the long-term ramifications might be far more important to society as a whole. What we've learned from the ethical blunders of executive leaders in politics, banking, housing, and technology is that everyone suffers from their ethical misconduct. This suffering takes the form of unemployment and economic disparity, polarization in our political discourse, and the degradation of the general welfare of society. In an uncertain world, viable success is dependent on the quality of a leader's character and how they actively nurture the values and purpose of the institution through their programs of education, training, and how they execute their mission.

Individual: Live a Character Based Leader Identity

On the individual level, character development is about your leader identity - the confidence, competence, and commitment to lead and win in any situation. Leaders facilitate and encourage **self-awareness**, **self-development**, and **lifelong learning** as the **coach**, **teacher**, and **mentor**. Through their actions they reinforce **resilience** at the individual and team level to persevere through difficult times.

It begins with self-awareness. Many people don't know their personal values (the WHO) or their purpose (the WHY). As you read this, could you articulate your own values and purpose? Don't be alarmed if you can't. True self-awareness can be more challenging than you think. Honest reflection can be a difficult and uncomfortable process, but it is important to see yourself to understand how you fit into the team and identify with your tribe.

Leaders can't change a person's character, but they can nurture and develop it. Leaders and direct reports co-create strategies and set individual performance objectives that honor their values, support their purpose, and align with the duties of their job. This alignment enables the individual to self-actualize in a manner consistent with the character identity of the organization. Leaders encourage and reinforce the individual's intrinsic drive to be their best.

Intrinsic forms of motivation are anabolic. This means that intrinsic motivation provides energy to counteract the drain of stress from a crisis. As an internal drive, it is an efficient resource to provide confidence for a positive outcome, competence to find creative solutions, and the commitment to win. Understanding your leader identity and how to tap into your internal drive makes you remarkably resilient in extremely difficult situations. There is a calming reassurance in knowing you are doing what you believe to be the "right thing." People look to leaders for guidance during a crisis, and leaders look to their values and purpose to provide that guidance. This is how leaders fill the cup of their personal resilience to meet the burden of the leadership moment.

Building a character identity for any organization requires work. It has to be the priority. Your shared values and common purpose provide clarity through ambiguity, confidence in times of uncertainty, and a commitment to weather the volatility of any storm. From this character identity, you can leverage the intrinsic forms of motivation so critical to find and implement creative solutions to VUCA problems. Character is a human quality, and therefore, people must come first. If you want an inspired, driven, and committed workforce, then your organization can benefit from the Character Alignment Methodology. This is the foundation for organizations to thrive and win in the modern VUCA reality.

Concept Summary: Align Values and Purpose to Inspire Performance

If we really want to get to know someone, we need to understand their values (the WHO) and their purpose (the WHY). Asking these questions requires a certain intimacy and vulnerability, but the answers reveal the most authentic qualities of a person's identity. Collectively, these qualities shape the living essence of an organization. Forging a strong character in your team builds clarity, confidence, and commitment to persevere through the stress and ambiguity of today's problems and tomorrow's challenges.

The Character Alignment Methodology harnesses the intrinsic drive of your people for a stronger team. Intrinsic motivation is the most effective, efficient, and sustainable way to discover meaningful solutions to seemingly impossible problems. Inspired people want to be better versions of themselves. Promoting self-awareness and alignment to shared values and a common purpose sets the conditions for each team member to self-actualize in a manner that achieves organizational outcomes. When people strive to be better, they make the team better. Regardless of the obstacle or setback, shared values and a common purpose allow your team to regroup, reorient, and harness their full potential to win in any environment.

When an organization looks inward to build a team based on character, the values and purpose provide a solid foundation to guide behaviors, decisions, and actions. To achieve sustainable results in our modern VUCA reality, the means are as important - if not more so - than the ends. We want to achieve the right things, but we have a social obligation to do it the right way. The qualities of your

47

people and how you align those qualities to the character and intentions of the organization matter. The Character Alignment Methodology provides a way to do that through mutually supporting efforts from the institution (culture), the leaders across the organization (climate), and the individual (identity).

Considerations to Align Values and Purpose to Inspire Performance

The following questions provide a method to assess strengths and potential areas of growth to achieve Alignment in the ADAPT Framework:

- How is your desired character identity (values and purpose) *actively* integrated into the human resources processes of the organization (Institution, Organization, and Individual) to include hiring and recruiting, counseling, and performance assessment and review?

- Because character alignment requires self-awareness, what steps are you taking to help people identify their individual values (the WHO), unique purpose (the WHY), and understand how these qualities align to the shared values and common purpose of the organization?

- How does your organization champion positive examples of your character identity in action, and conversely, how efficient and effective is the organization in addressing unethical behavior or activities that are inconsistent with the shared values and common purpose for the organization?

- How does your organization invest in character development to include awareness, experiential learning, application, and reinforcement on both an individual and collective level?

- How does the organization use feedback mechanisms to review and assess its commitment to the shared values and common purpose of its character identity?

6 | DEVELOP CAMARADERIE FOR STRONGER TEAMS

I am a member of a team, and I rely on the team. I defer to it and sacrifice for it, because the team, not the individual, is the ultimate champion.

- Mia Hamm

Camaraderie is an indelible quality of the military culture. This makes sense given the common purpose, shared hardship, and personal sacrifice of the military experience. Throughout history, camaraderie has been an intangible yet decisive factor in shaping the outcomes of battles, campaigns, and even wars. Military units benefit from camaraderie during the most challenging times, but leaders actually develop camaraderie for stronger teams well before the shooting starts. Combat may immortalize the relationships for the band of brothers and sisters, but it is certainly not necessary to forge those relationships.

By definition, camaraderie is the mutual trust and fellowship among people who spend a lot of time together. It describes a deeper mental, emotional, and even spiritual connection shared by members of a team. These connections create a synergy where the whole is greater than the sum of the parts by inspiring individuals to give their full measure of talent and effort to the team. In many cases, that team becomes a family. Camaraderie elevates ordinary teams to do extraordinary things. We refer to the epic victory of the 1980 U.S. Olympic Hockey team over the Soviet Union as the "Miracle on Ice" for a reason. Camaraderie provides every underdog the opportunity to become a champion.

The underdog turned champion can be your story. In this chapter, we describe how the military develops camaraderie through their onboarding process as an application of the Self-Determination Theory, and we also explore how leaders develop camaraderie using the Gap to Growth Leadership Approach. With these proven strategies, you can develop camaraderie for a stronger team to overcome the most daunting challenges in the modern VUCA reality.

Applying the Self-Determination Theory during the Onboarding Process

Incentives may bring people into an organization, but that isn't what makes them stay. During a crisis, we have to rely on our people - their confidence, competence, and commitment to find a way to win. When we talk about camaraderie, we are talking about that commitment to the team, the mission, but - most importantly - each other. If you wait until a crisis to develop camaraderie, you're too late. The best place to start is at the beginning - when new employees first show up in your organization.

The military has a ritual to initiate new recruits into the warrior culture. We call it basic training. The mythical stories shared from this experience are woven into the legend and lore of the military journey. You might recognize the screaming drill instructor, harsh discipline, grueling schedule, and other forms of hazing as some of the more familiar vignettes of basic training. Every service member is initiated through this ritual, and every veteran has a basic training story. It represents the transformation from civilian to warrior, someone committed to the identity of an institution with a common set of values and shared purpose. Imagine what your team could achieve if you began developing that sense of camaraderie the very first day a new employee shows up at your organization.

We are not suggesting that you adopt military rituals as part of your onboarding process. That form of initiation is best kept in the military. The specifics of what the military does isn't as important as the psychology behind how it works. The military's onboarding process is an application of the Self-Determination Theory. Once you understand the psychology, you can develop your own culturally appropriate rituals for your organization.

Richard Ryan and Edward Deci are the two psychologists that developed the **Self-Determination Theory** to describe the continuum of behavior from extrinsic forms of motivation (the carrots and sticks) to intrinsic forms of motivation (personal drive to self-actualization). This continuum and how it applies to the military is reflected in Figure 7. Based on this theory, personal growth depends on three mutually supporting motivations: competence, relatedness or connection, and autonomy.[58] Let's explore how basic training walks through this process to create that shared identity essential for camaraderie.

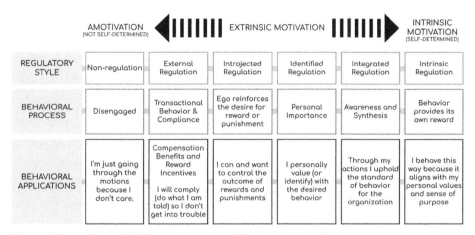

Figure 7. Applied Self-Determination Theory to understand the continuum of behavior from extrinsic to intrinsic forms of motivation[59]

The military leverages a comprehensive program of incentives to attract new recruits. College tuition, specialty training, monetary bonuses, competitive salaries, health benefits, and life insurance provide the external rewards that entice young men and women to volunteer for military service. Once new recruits report for basic training, they are subjected to a program of indoctrination that conditions behavior to the standards and norms of the military institution. At this stage, compliance is the desired outcome. This exemplifies *external regulation*: Do what you're told, when you're told, or face some unpleasant consequences.

After this initial shock, new trainees exercise *introjected regulation* - they move right along the continuum of the Self-Determination Theory. The trainee savors the small victories that come doing the little things right. It could be something as simple as accomplishing a facing movement, wearing the uniform correctly, or keeping up with the rest of the unit during a formation run. Doing these things correctly keeps them from attracting negative attention. Because anxiety and the fear of consequences motivates behavior, the motivation is still extrinsic. Any positive acknowledgement validates and motivates future behavior. The important distinction with introjected regulation is the individual's recognition that they are responsible for whether or not their actions invite the external rewards (praise) or punishments (admonishment).

The military has a reputation for breaking individuals down and building them up again. What's really going on is - over time - the individual comes to value those behaviors that align with the expected and implied norms of their unit. The basic training experience has a conditioning effect reinforcing the values and deeper purpose of the institution. Through *identified regulation*, members of the team begin to identify with the shared qualities of their group specifically and the institution more broadly. They march in formation. They shout unit mottos with pride. They relate to one another and begin to recognize their distinctiveness from those outside the group. Belonging is its own reward, and trainees commit to behaviors and activities worthy of membership.

Over time, the individual internalizes the standards of behavior as their own. With *integrated regulation*, values, purpose, and identity of the individual achieves synthesis with the values, purpose, and identity of the group. There is a conscious alignment between organizational norms and personal behavior. Service members adhere to military standards both on and off duty. They feel an intrinsic impulse, a constant reminder of who they are and what they represent. Every service member acknowledges they are a reflection of the institution through their personal example, and they share in the pride of being recognized as part of the military community.

Graduation from basic training provides a foundation for what happens next. Once the individual has completed their initiation, they are ready for the next challenge of their military adventure. This is why it's called "basic" training. It's just the first step. More difficult challenges and opportunities await. Now they are members of an exclusive tribe. Any activity that furthers competence, confidence, or commitment to the shared values and purpose of the institution becomes its own reward. The drive is internal. Individuals feel a personal sense of satisfaction when they put forth their best effort for the group, and likewise, they share in the sense of accomplishment that comes from the success of their unit. They inherently strive for self-actualization because of what it means to the success of the team. Others are counting on them. They want to do their part.

Once the motivation shifts from external incentives to the internal drive, we unleash the power of inspired behaviors.

Competence, relatedness, and autonomy lead to enhanced self-motivation and psychological well-being in the Self-Determination Theory. It starts with basic training, and subsequent assignments along the military journey provide new opportunities to demonstrate competence of mastering tasks with increasing difficulty. Relatedness comes from the sense of belonging to the team and a shared commitment to something meaningful. With each level of mastery comes more responsibility - and more autonomy. Once leaders in the army have mastered the platoon (between 10 and 40 soldiers), they command the company (between 40 and 200 soldiers). After company level leadership comes the chance to lead at the battalion level (between 200 and 800 soldiers) - and so on. Through this cyclical construct, the military harnesses the motivation and internal drive towards self-actualization to achieve higher performance outcomes for the group.

Remember, this process began with the promise of external rewards. Education benefits, job training, and healthcare are a means to an end. The unique onboarding process pushes individuals from left to right along the continuum from extrinsic to intrinsic forms of motivation. At its culmination, recruits no longer see themselves as civilians. They are soldiers, sailors, airmen, or marines. The military is no longer a means but an end in and of itself. This is how a four-year service obligation turns into a twenty-year career. This progression is made possible because the organization assumes an active role in shifting motivation along the continuum of self-determination.

Similarly, nonmilitary organizations attract talent with competitive compensation and benefits packages. Just like the incentives that attract new recruits into the military, these carrots bring people into the organization. If you stop there along the continuum, so does the individual. Their behavior will be motivated by carrots and sticks. If the best you can offer are incentives or rewards, then as soon as someone else offers a bigger carrot, that employee will leave. If the organization assumes no responsibility in how they manage motivation, individuals can remain stuck or even regress backwards into a state of amotivation. In other words, they become disengaged and dissociated. You might recognize these employees as the ones who stare at the clock or go through the motions until they can escape the confines of their workspace at the earliest opportunity.

Amotivation describes the state of engagement for the largest segment of the U.S. workforce today. Furthermore, behavior managed by rewards and punishments cannot survive in the modern VUCA reality. When the crisis deprives an organization of its resources (the carrots), managers are left with only the authority of their position (the stick) to compel behavior. This invokes a culture of fear. Toxic environments suppress the qualities of creativity, curiosity, commitment, and drive essential to thrive and win during a crisis. In these environments, people don't care about performance. They only care about survival. The group construct collapses. Organizations can't achieve their collective potential while everyone in the workspace is struggling to survive.

Self-Determination Theory describes a process to forge a shared identity along a continuum of behaviors from extrinsic to intrinsic motivations. This is how individuals become a team, and how that team becomes a family. You don't need a program like basic training to make this happen. You just need to understand the psychology. So, how do you align individual values and purpose to the shared values and collective purpose of the team? How do you shape a shared identity with new members of your team? How do you actively shift from a program of incentives to create an inspired workforce? How are you working to make your team more than just the sum of individual parts to achieve and win in the modern VUCA reality?

Building High Performance Teams

What happens after basic training? After forging a cohesive group of trainees with a shared identity, the military breaks up the team. Basic training graduates are sent to new units, and after another two to four years, the military moves them again. This seems contrary to what you might expect after investing all the time and resources to build camaraderie through the onboarding process. Basic training introduces camaraderie and forges the individual's identity and commitment to the institution. Leaders at the military unit take it from there to shape that identity and build camaraderie in the unit. We've defined that process as the Gap to Growth (GTG) Leadership Approach to help you build that sense of camaraderie for your team.

The **GTG Leadership Approach** is conceptually based on Abraham Maslow's Hierarchy of Needs (see Figure 8). The nature of individual motivation serves as the underlying premise and focus for leader engagement. Physiological and safety requirements are basic needs - food, clothing, water, shelter, and security. These needs come first. Belonging - a sense of relatedness and social connection, and esteem - the measure of self-worth - are psychological needs. These motivations come after the basic needs are met. Atop this Hierarchy of Needs is the motivation for personal growth and self-actualization. This is where leaders want their people to be in high performance organizations.

Both the basic and psychological tiers in this hierarchy are classified as deficiency needs. If any of these needs are not met, they create a gap along an individual's path to achieve self-actualization. Self-actualization is the only growth need. **Only when basic needs are met can an individual satisfy their psychological needs, and only when an individual satisfies their psychological needs can they pursue growth toward self-actualization.** The GTG Leadership Approach is where leaders fill the gaps along this hierarchy to open a path to self-actualization. Along the way they build trust, create a shared sense of identity, and foster a deep sense of camaraderie.

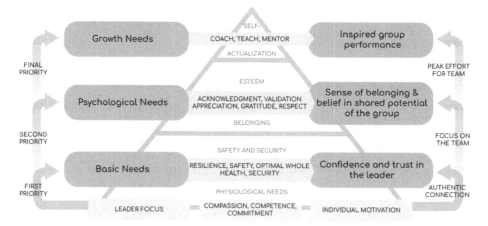

Figure 8. The Gap to Growth (GTG) Leadership Approach is an active leadership application using Maslow's Hierarchy of Needs

Basic Needs Leadership: Putting the Needs of Others First

Leaders eat last. This is a fundamental lesson of military leadership. Simon Sinek leveraged this implicit norm from the military culture as the theme to his bestselling book: *Leaders Eat Last: Why Some Teams Pull Together and Others Don't.* The premise is simple: **When leaders tend to the needs of their people, those people can direct their energy to the larger needs of the team.** When it's time to eat in the military, leaders stand in the back of the chow line to ensure their subordinates get served before tending to their own plate. If there is not enough food, then the leader goes hungry. This symbolic act demonstrates the leader's commitment to the needs of their subordinates.

Another way military leaders show commitment to their people relates to safety and security - another basic need in Maslow's Hierarchy. Commanders stand in front of their formation both physically and metaphorically. They don't hide behind the cover and concealment of their people. They are the first exposed to the danger of whatever threat lies before the team. This sounds like an act of

58

courage, but it is also an act of compassion. Shared hardship helps leaders understand how to best care for and protect their people.

Standing in front of the formation means leaders are accountable for any and all outcomes - particularly when things go wrong. In the army, there is a regulation that stipulates commanders are responsible for everything the organization does or fails to do.[60] That means everything, successes and failures. Regulations prohibit a commander from transferring blame. This punitive standard forces leaders to ensure their people have what they need to succeed (security, protection, education, training, information, resources, etc.), because they don't have the luxury to point fingers if the unit fails.

Commitment and compassion alone are not enough. Leaders must also be competent. In addition to a willingness to wait at the back of the line when it's time to eat, they must also have the wherewithal to provide the food. They don't have to cook, but they do need a viable solution to satisfy their team's need to eat. More than just feeling compassion when times are hard, they must demonstrate the ability to make things better. Through their example, they persevere and encourage others to do the same in otherwise desperate moments. This is particularly true under the harsh conditions of a deployment environment. Regardless of the situation, military leaders are expected to find a way to win. This is why leaders are always learning and growing - especially in the VUCA environment.

Let's consider how this plays out in a nonmilitary setting. Compensation and job security provide the means for basic needs in a civilian context. By this analogy, leaders take their share only after subordinate employees have had theirs. When there isn't enough to go around, the executives make the first sacrifice. This means no stock payouts, severance packages, or bonuses during hard times. Layoffs come after the c-suite has depleted its coffers. As leaders, they eat last.

It also means the leader is the first to face the fire during a crisis in the same way a commander leads from the front in combat. If employees are expected to return to work during a pandemic, their leader is the first one through the door. When the organization struggles, the leader accepts the responsibility and faces any consequences. The proverbial buck stops at the top. It doesn't roll downhill.

A leader's concern is not for themselves or their shareholders. It is for the people - *their* people. If the people are taken care of, the rest takes care of itself. Trust and faith are reciprocal qualities. Subordinates must trust and have faith in their leader, and the leader must trust and have faith in their people. If this doesn't sound like privilege coming from position or stature, it's because leadership has nothing to do with privilege or stature. *True* leadership is a burden.

The magnitude of this burden in the VUCA reality will expose a manager or executive's true intentions. Anyone can commit to protect and care for their people when there is no risk in doing so. That's easy. The real question is: *What are you willing to do - to give of yourself - when times are hard?* Are you willing to put the needs of others ahead of your own? Are you willing to eat last - take your share only after everyone else has had their fill? Are you willing to be vulnerable and expose yourself by standing in front of your people? If you have the courage to do that, people will trust and follow you. This is what it means to lead.

The combination of commitment, compassion, and competence from the leader engenders trust and confidence from the people. They earn that trust because they help satisfy an individual's most essential needs. In doing so, the members of your team aren't preoccupied with survival. They can focus on higher order needs. When you focus on your people, your people can focus on the team. This is the first step to develop camaraderie.

Psychological Needs Leadership: Building Teams and Organizational Momentum

Once the basic needs are met, people can set intentions toward the psychological needs of belonging and esteem in Maslow's Hierarchy. Belonging is a remarkably human quality. It has nothing to do with rank or anything worn on the uniform. We are all inherently social beings whether we are wearing a military uniform or business casual. The open-loop nature of our limbic system means we are more than just open to emotional connection. We crave it. Our psychological health depends on it. When we have a sense of belonging, connection, and respect, we experience the happiness that comes from the release of serotonin and oxytocin. We *feel* connected. We *feel* like we belong. In order to develop camaraderie, leaders set the conditions for everyone to experience belonging and esteem.

Leaders start by creating a distinct - yet meaningful - identity for the team. Remember, the military moves people to new duty stations every few years. Team building is an ongoing challenge as commanders work to integrate new people with unique backgrounds, experiences, and qualifications. This challenge is made harder because even within the military, many subgroups exist. The military has a way of parceling one group from another based on mission, experience, qualifications, or a combination of all three. These distinctions are reflected by what is worn on the uniform. Aviators have pilot wings. Navy SEALS wear the coveted trident. Marines have the Eagle, Globe, and Anchor. Paratroopers wear red berets and airborne wings. Combat veterans wear a unit patch on their right shoulder. Everyone wears rank insignia. We have so many ways of distinguishing the role and identity of service members wearing the same uniform, it makes you wonder how it is even possible to create a shared identity and sense of belonging for a specific unit.

So what's the answer? Well, the methodology for building high performance teams has less to do with what's on the uniform than it does with who's wearing the uniform. Because emotions occur on a subconscious level, a leader's authenticity matters. The leader has to be genuine, and they have to demonstrate vulnerability to show their "human" side. Crazy, right? Soldiers and sailors vulnerable? Leaders must be confident in their own identity (values and purpose) and also need a measure of emotional courage to step out from behind the uniform to let subordinates see them for who they are as a person. This is how leaders make meaningful - yet appropriate - connections with their subordinates. Service members obey orders based on rank, but before they willingly follow a leader, they must identify with the person. A commitment to vulnerability provides the humility and honest empathy to meet people where they are, make a connection, and then motivate them to where they need to be.

Brené Brown, a research professor at the University of Houston who has spent two decades studying courage, vulnerability, shame, and empathy, explains, "Vulnerability is not about winning or losing. It's having the courage to show up even when you can't control the outcome."[61] Vulnerability is the key to building the intimacy essential for trust and camaraderie. It is a quality that leaders in the military learn through the example of others. Leaders have to disarm the protective impulse of their ego to make genuine, human connections. More importantly, they have to create a safe and non-judgmental environment for members of the team to make these same connections with one another.

This isn't easy, but the nature of the military experience provides ample opportunities for service members to see each other as human beings. Mortal stakes have a way of blasting through any protective shell to expose the frailty of our nature. On combat deployments, we see each other at our best, our worst, and even our ugliest. When we feel exposed, we rely on our comrades for cover because we have to. In return, we provide them cover. Despite our vulnerability, we come together as one because we are safer, stronger, and better that way.

You don't need the same life or death stakes to understand the value of camaraderie, but you do need to meet the psychological requirements of belonging and esteem. In 2012, Google conducted a multi-year study called "Project Aristotle," a quest to build the perfect team. Surprisingly, the number one finding of the results was psychological safety. "The behaviors that create psychological safety — conversational turn-taking and empathy — are part of the same unwritten rules we often turn to, as individuals, when we need to establish a bond. And those human bonds matter as much at work as anywhere else. In fact, they sometimes matter more."[62] Vulnerability can be expressed or experienced by anyone at any time. It describes the uncertainty, risk, and emotional exposure of genuine human interaction.[63] You just need the courage to show up. This requires a mastery of emotional intelligence to navigate personal and professional boundaries in an appropriate, positive way.

These are personal connections for professional relationships. They aren't friendships, but they share some of the same qualities. The key difference is in the selfless nature of the relationship. They aren't transactional exchanges of emotion.

There is a great deal of compassion, but each person recognizes and respects the deeper values and purpose of the institution. Taking care of others in a manner consistent with those values and purpose is how you take care of yourself *and* the mission. The benefits you receive are given on faith in the same way that people place their faith in your leadership. Any violation of this sacred arrangement is an affront to the institution and a betrayal of the team. When you build a team like this, looking out for one another becomes an intuitive quality - an instinct that resembles the behaviors of a close-knit family but grounded in the shared values and purpose of the institution.

Practically speaking, this means blurring the boundaries between our personal and professional lives. When appropriate, the entire team participates in the celebration of personal achievements and milestones such as graduations, engagements, weddings, birthdays, and holidays. It also means the entire team supports each other during moments of hardship or times of grief. The team shows up for a family member's funeral. They raise money for a colleague's sick child. They provide meals for a coworker's family after a tragedy. Finally, in moments where a member of the team experiences disappointment or shame, we offer compassion instead of judgment. We accept the fallibility of human nature, and in that shared space of personal vulnerability, we connect on a deeper level. We see ourselves in each other, and we become a family.

Vulnerable moments outside the uniform are what forge the meaningful connections for what happens in the uniform. You'll know when you've achieved this level of connection when subordinates admit they "identify" with the leader and the team. The tipping point when a team becomes a family is the moment when its members feel such a commitment to each other that they fear disappointing the team more than failing the mission. Remember, what keeps the soldier in the foxhole isn't the mission. It is because their brother or sister is right there with them. They aren't fighting for the mission. They are fighting for each other.

Once you've achieved belonging, the next gap involves esteem. The leader reinforces self-worth through a combination of acknowledgement, validation, appreciation, gratitude, and respect. The leader can do this by setting incremental, achievable goals and then celebrating those accomplishments on both an organizational and individual level.

Everyone wants to be part of a winning team. Nobody likes to lose. Incremental objectives that are challenging but still within the capabilities of the team have the potential to generate inertia for learning, growth, and achievement. Stacking a series of wins creates momentum. Leaders infuse a sense of confidence in the individual and the collective competence in the team. Over time, optimism replaces anxiety. Eventually, people crave the most difficult challenge. It's not the cause that motivates them, it's the possibility of uncovering what lies beyond the horizon of their known potential.

Equally important to stacking wins is taking the time to celebrate those wins. Accomplishment provides an opportunity for leaders to reinforce self-worth and esteem by recognizing contributions to the winning effort in a *sincere* way. It doesn't help to call yourself a winner when you're losing every game or always failing to achieve your objectives. Participation trophies only go so far. Provided there is a valid accomplishment, leaders acknowledge and recognize contributions to the overall effort, and when the team doesn't succeed, leaders bounce back. They learn from mistakes and set intentions to be better the next time.

Building esteem requires leaders to show respect, fairness, and honest gratitude. They cannot have any ulterior motives. Explicit or implicit marginalization through nepotism, favoritism, fraternization, discrimination, harassment or other self-serving behaviors is inconsistent with the leader's sacred commitment to the welfare and success of their people. These behaviors will undermine any commitment the people might have for the team. Character is the mortar that holds a team together, and without it, the team will fall apart.

Engaged leaders set objectives and recognize efforts that bring the team together. Vapid praise or misplaced recognition could achieve the opposite effect. Individuals who believe their efforts go unnoticed could become resentful or disengaged. If objectives aren't challenging, your team could get complacent. They might even get too comfortable. When a crisis hits, there is a good chance they will be caught off guard. Growth is meant to be uncomfortable. Constantly increasing the level of difficulty keeps everyone on their toes. As the leader, keep your finger on the pulse of the team to assess their confidence and esteem so that you can apply the appropriate balance of challenge and support. Through this process, you can condition your team to be remarkably comfortable in otherwise uncomfortable situations.

Building the relationships that optimize individual potential and team achievement is how leaders develop camaraderie for stronger teams. Here is where the idea of "me" becomes "we" in the context of belonging and esteem. Service members don't just identify themselves as different from civilian society. They see themselves as better - not because of anything they can do on their own, but because of who stands next to them. Synergy expands individual capacity and capability to do and achieve more. The team becomes a family. The more the individual can give to his or her family, the more the family reciprocates in terms of love, appreciation, and achievement. They consider mere recognition as part of the team a distinct privilege and validation of their worth and potential.

Growth Needs Leadership: Coach, Teach, Mentor toward Self-Actualization

Once the basic and psychological needs are met, you can address the individual growth needs across the organization. Inspired behavior is the desired outcome. To do this, leaders act as the coach, teacher, and mentor. Some employees might require coaching to set challenging goals or find direction. Some might require teaching to gain knowledge or learn new skills. Still others might need the advice and guidance from a mentor. Your job is to address those growth needs on an individual level. When your people perform at their best, the team performs at its best. The coach, teach, and mentor approach is a personalized means to optimize individual performance to achieve organizational results (we will discuss the specifics of the Coach-Teach-Mentor Methodology in greater detail later).

Leaders take this to scale through their personal example. If they want others to be inspired, they must be inspired themselves. They provide the source of positive energy for the organization. As the leader, you set the tone for the organization's climate. The way you engage, counsel, and support subordinate leaders sets the example that trickles down and expands across the team. With the GTG Leadership Approach, leaders are constantly assessing individual and collective needs of the organization and balancing strategies to meet those needs. In this construct, effective leadership is never about the mission. It is always about the people. This is how it works in the most elite military units.

Focusing on the people is hard. Really hard. The personal energy required to make meaningful connections across a diverse group of people with individual needs to create a shared identity and then direct that group toward a common objective isn't easy. No two people have the same deficiency needs. Vulnerability requires courage. Selflessness requires commitment. Everyone has unique growth needs. It seems like it would be much easier to infer the quality of leadership based on organizational results. Because real leadership is hard, many organizations choose that expedient, practical option by assuming the effectiveness of leadership based on bottom line results. Unfortunately, the easy button doesn't work in the VUCA environment.

Develop Camaraderie for Stronger Teams Concept Summary

What we are learning through workforce surveys and employee feedback is that the logic of inferring effective leadership based exclusively on bottom-line results is flawed - particularly in the VUCA reality. Without camaraderie, an organization may survive under "normal" conditions. They may even be profitable. With enough incentives, you can keep an organization running. However, without individual commitment to a shared identity, the team lacks the durability or resilience to withstand the pressure of a crisis. If the leader doesn't commit to address basic or psychological needs, human nature tells us that people will tend to them on their own. The majority of our modern workforce feels disconnected because they don't trust their leaders to satisfy their basic needs, psychological needs, or growth needs - particularly during a crisis.

In the military, camaraderie is forged in times of peace so that the team comes together as something more during times of war. It starts during basic training -

the military's version of employee onboarding. Applying the Self-Determination Theory, the psychology of the onboarding process facilitates connection, growth, and autonomy to unleash intrinsically motivated behaviors so that people strive to become better. Better people become better service members. Camaraderie leverages our sociability as fuel for the drive toward higher performance outcomes.

In a nonmilitary context, a culture of camaraderie has the potential to turn an ordinary organization into a tight-knit team of dependable, reliable, and committed members of a family. As a family, this band of brothers and sisters closes ranks when threatened. From the people is where the organization draws its strength to persevere and thrive in the VUCA environment. The people are the only constant, and therefore, the spendthrift act that focuses on the people is the only practical choice. Camaraderie has the power to turn an underdog into a champion.

The Gap to Growth Leadership Approach (GTG) provides a framework to understand how leaders transform an organization of capable individuals into a confident, competent, and committed team. When the leader provides a combination of commitment, compassion, and competence to meet basic needs, individuals feel a sense of trust and confidence in their leader. More importantly, they can focus their energy on the psychological needs of belonging and esteem. Vulnerability and authenticity forge a deep commitment analogous to the connections that bind the members of a family. By generating inertia toward learning and growth through incremental wins, the team gains confidence in their ability to handle the most complex and unforeseen problems. Finally, the leader acts as the coach, teacher, and mentor to inspire higher levels of individual performance. Camaraderie is achieved when people focus their energy and talent for the good of the group, because they recognize their well-being and success is inextricably linked to well-being and success of the team. The team best positioned to thrive in the VUCA environment is the one where its members are inspired to perform at their best for the collective good of everyone on the team.

Considerations to Develop Camaraderie for Stronger Teams

The following questions provide a method to assess strengths and potential areas of growth to develop the culture of camaraderie in the ADAPT Framework:

- How does your organization's onboarding process connect individual values and purpose to create a shared identity for the team?

- What are the explicit and implicit norms that guide behavior and distinguish group identity from external organizations?

- How do leaders demonstrate commitment, compassion, and competence when it comes to meeting the basic needs of their employees?

- How engaged is the organization in celebrating personal milestones and supporting families during times of hardship?

- How does the organization balance competence and confidence in generating momentum from incremental wins through acknowledgment, validation, appreciation, gratitude, and respect?

7 | APPLY THE HIERARCHY OF ORGANIZATIONAL AGILITY

Don't tell people how to do things, tell them what to do and let them surprise you with their results.

-    General George Patton

For our part, we happened to be in the right place at the right time. It was the middle of summer, the time of year with the most intense fighting in Afghanistan. The original mission for our crew was to set up MEDEVAC coverage at a remote forward operating base (FOB) in the Farah Province. The proposed location was about 250 miles west of our base in Kandahar. Our task was to validate the inclement weather recovery procedures with our UH60 helicopter and to assess the facilities at the FOB to stage a MEDEVAC capability there.

We were expanding MEDEVAC because the level of violence across the country had begun to spiral out of control. Casualty numbers were up - way up, and many partners from the 50-nation coalition were packing their bags and heading back home. Cracks were beginning to form in the solidarity so prominent across the coalition in the wake of the 9/11 terrorist attacks. An extended war with increasing costs just wasn't what our allies signed up for. As the Afghan forces expanded operations across the country, we had to reduce the incidence and severity of casualties. This was made harder by the fact that it was extremely dangerous to travel on the handful of improved roads across the country. More attacks on the ground meant more evacuations by air. It's hard to argue improvements in security and stability while the death toll is skyrocketing. To address this challenge, our job was to complete the coordination to expand MEDEVAC coverage into the westernmost regions of the country.

This was one of the easiest missions in a combat environment. After we flew a few terminal instrument approach procedures, we landed at the FOB to tour the facilities. Once we were finished, we were checking the weather for the return flight to Kandahar when we were approached by the senior U.S. representative on the base. She received a distress call from a convoy that was ambushed on the highway north of our location. They had wounded personnel. Some were in critical condition. The nearest medical facility was at our current location. Given the terrain, the convoy was at least 90 minutes away by ground, and that was the best case scenario. The nature of the injuries suggested they didn't have that much time.

It's important to note that MEDEVAC wasn't our mission. We weren't a MEDEVAC aircraft, and we didn't have the crew or equipment to provide lifesaving care. We didn't have a red cross on the side of our aircraft, and we were not authorized to conduct an evacuation mission. As often happens in combat, circumstances have a tendency to unfold in unpredictable ways. The simple fact was that the wounded had to be evacuated by air, and we were the only capable helicopter available for hundreds of miles. The clock was ticking.

Any decision to evacuate casualties by air wasn't an easy one. Helicopters were high value targets in Afghanistan. Losing a helicopter in combat was front page news. We knew this. So did the enemy. Insurgents would routinely bait aircraft into ambush sites. This was particularly true for any MEDEVAC because the Red Cross on the side of the fuselage meant the aircraft was unarmed. The enemy could shoot at these helicopters all day without the fear of them shooting back. In addition to machine gun fire and rocket propelled grenades, insurgents planted improvised explosive devices in potential landing sites. They strung wire in trees to trigger explosions from the helicopter's rotor wash. Evacuating casualties had become our most important, most vulnerable, and most dangerous mission in Afghanistan.

Getting the right permission for any MEDEVAC was an involved process. Aviation was a constrained resource that was intensely managed at the most senior levels of command. In order to get authorization to evacuate these casualties, we would have to contact our commander back in Kandahar who would then have to contact the U.S. Headquarters in Bagram. We tried that. Our commander wasn't available, so we attempted to notify the U.S. command in Bagram directly. That didn't work either. The people who could give us the thumbs up weren't available, and we didn't have time to wait. We did understand the deeper purpose of why we were in Farah in the first place. We knew the intent. We were there to save lives, and in this situation, that was exactly what we were going to do.

We weren't a MEDEVAC aircraft and crew, but that didn't matter. All we needed to do was fly out to the location of the attack, load the casualties, and deliver them to medical care in Farah. We could do that. We chose a route and approach to minimize our exposure and reduce the risk. Our abbreviated crew briefing was our way of applying discipline to our initiative. Within minutes, we were off the ground and on our way to the site of the attack.

It didn't take long to get there, but by the time we did, the fight was over. There was one damaged vehicle burning by the side of the road. We could see the scattered debris and other evidence of a firefight. The U.S. element popped smoke when they saw our aircraft so we could identify the site of the wounded. We circled to land in the high dust environment. We were only on the ground for a minute. We loaded the casualties and were on our way back to Farah before the dust cleared. The entire flight there and back took less than 20 minutes. Once we offloaded the casualties at the medical treatment facility, we took off and headed east toward Kandahar.

All things considered; it was an uneventful flight. It was a relatively easy mission. Nobody shot at us. In fact, we didn't see any enemy at all. We executed a mission we were not authorized to do in a completely unfamiliar area. *Because we had a shared understanding of the intent, we took the initiative. We acted on our own using our best judgment.*

We were almost 20 minutes into our flight back to Kandahar when we received a relayed call from Bagram authorizing us to do the mission we had just completed. Over an hour had passed since we made the decision to act on our own. Shortly thereafter, we received a follow-up call from Farah telling us that the wounded soldier was going to survive. If we had followed protocol and waited for approval, the outcome would have been much different. We acted on our own initiative to do the mission. We had the best perspective to make the most informed decision, so we did. We had the agility to act decisively, and we saved a life.

An organization becomes more agile by applying a hierarchy of behaviors that empowers individuals to take the initiative under a prudent level of risk. The army calls this mission command. In this chapter, we will compare mission command to the behavioral model of VUCA Prime to validate its application for nonmilitary purposes. Furthermore, we will outline the Hierarchy of Organizational Agility to describe how leaders, like you, create agile organizations that act decisively to seize opportunities in the VUCA reality.

The Relationship between Mission Command and VUCA Prime

Mission command is a military term that describes how leaders empower subordinate decision making for decentralized execution appropriate to the situation.[64] This is how army units become more agile in fluid environments. It means that all players on the team understand the leader's vision and their part in turning that vision into reality. Mission command encourages initiative and innovation to seek out and take advantage of opportunities in situations with a high degree of uncertainty and ambiguity - like the casualty evacuation example provided earlier. **This is how you give power to your people.**

To understand how to apply mission command to your organization, let's examine a similar nonmilitary framework, VUCA Prime, created by Robert Johansen, a distinguished fellow at the Institute for the Future in Silicon Valley. VUCA Prime is a behavioral model for an active response to VUCA conditions through a combination of vision, understanding, clarity, and agility. You can see how the principles of mission command align with each element of VUCA Prime in Figure 9.

COMPARING PRINCIPLES OF MISSION COMMAND TO THE ELEMENTS OF VUCA PRIME	
THE PRINCIPLES OF MISSION COMMAND[65]	THE ELEMENTS OF VUCA PRIME[65]
Commander's Intent	Vision: Leaders stay focused on the desired target
Competence	Understanding: Explore and analyze the environment from multiple perspectives
Shared Understanding	
Mission Orders	Clarity: Recognize when and how to simplify and remove obstacles to make timely, effective decisions
Disciplined Initiative, Risk Acceptance, Mutual Trust	Agility: Be adaptive through collaboration, delivery, and reflection

Figure 9. Comparison between the army construct of Mission Command and the behavioral model of VUCA Prime

A key difference between the two models concerns the desired quality of agility. Mission command describes the actions and intentions your organization can take to become more agile, and VUCA Prime describes the concepts that - if present - allow you to counter the challenges of the modern VUCA reality. In VUCA Prime, agility is one of those qualities. VUCA Prime presumes that you already know how to be agile while mission command provides the framework to achieve that outcome.

A deeper understanding of mission command reveals a certain order of precedence in the principles necessary to achieve organizational agility. First, you need trust. Shared character grounds your people in values and purpose, and teams with strong camaraderie have - by definition - a high level of **mutual trust**. We covered each of these concepts in the Align and Develop parts of the ADAPT Framework. Second, you need intentional **competence** for growth through learning and increased capabilities through diversity and inclusion. These two principles provide a foundation for greater agility.

From that foundation, the leader communicates the intent - a clear, concise, yet comprehensive **vision** of what success looks like. From that vision, the staff analyzes potential solutions for coordinated action with decentralized execution and communicates those solutions in **mission orders**. During execution, leaders practice **risk acceptance** while subordinates - armed with the intent and mission orders for **shared understanding** - exercise **disciplined initiative** to take action as opportunities emerge. The combination of shared understanding, risk acceptance, and disciplined initiative toward a clear vision is how organizations become more agile in dynamic environments. We call the sequence of these activities the **Hierarchy of Organizational Agility.**

Understanding the Hierarchy of Organizational Agility

Organizational agility can be modeled in a manner similar to Maslow's Hierarchy of Needs. Foundation, vision, process, and dynamic operations describe the Hierarchy of Organizational Agility (see Figure 10). Each level builds upon a set of conditions to enable employees at all levels to act independently and decisively in any environment. The base of this hierarchy combines mutual trust and intentional competence. From this foundation, the organization works as a team to bring the leader's vision to life.

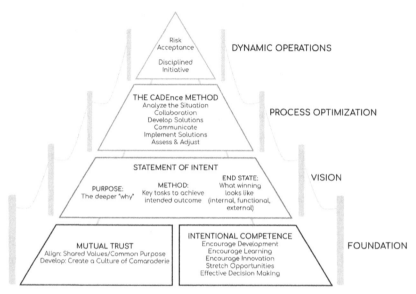

Figure 10. The Hierarchy of Organizational Agility describes behaviors that build upon each other empowering employees to act decisively in the face of the VUCA challenge.

With a clear and concise picture of what success looks like, the entire organization can focus its energy and resources toward that end state. Together, subordinate departments and business functions can analyze the situation, collaborate, develop solutions, communicate, implement solutions, and assess and adjust the plan as necessary. These activities empower employees to take action appropriate to the situation. Through the Hierarchy of Organizational Agility, everyone across the team from every business unit becomes an asset to move the organization toward the intended outcome.

Let's consider why it is necessary to describe agility through this hierarchy. Leaders won't empower employees they don't trust, and employees won't have any confidence to exercise initiative if they don't trust their leader. If an organization hopes to keep pace with unknown or unforeseen challenges, learning must be a continuous process that leaders prioritize and nurture across the organization. Leaders must be able to visualize, describe, and direct their intent so employees understand what they are doing and why they are doing it. From that statement of intent, the staff can apply a collaborative problem solving approach to develop coordinated solutions for decentralized execution. When the business functions and staff are aligned, they can streamline information and prioritize efforts for synchronized action across the organization. **At its peak, organizations become agile when individual employees have clarity, competence, and confidence to take action and their leaders are willing to accept the risk in doing so.**

Let's dive into how you and your organization can apply each element of the Hierarchy of Organizational Agility, starting with the bottom of the pyramid.

Setting the **Foundation** of Mutual Trust and Intentional Competence

The first two steps of the ADAPT Framework showcase how you establish a climate of **mutual trust.** Alignment connects individual values and purpose to an organization and culture that shares the same ideals and mission, and trusted relationships are a prerequisite to develop camaraderie for stronger teams. Mutual trust is essential, but it is a quality that only represents half of the foundation for the Hierarchy of Organizational Agility.

The second half of the foundation involves the concept of **intentional competence.** Competence is described as *intentional* because it is a process of active engagement. The goal is not about acquiring a specific knowledge or skill but *continued growth* and *learning.* Everybody in the organization is always seeking to learn, improve, and explore with a mind open for new opportunities to address complex problems. As the foundation for organizational agility, intentional competence is a responsibility shared on an individual level and with the team as a whole.

Individuals are empowered to be resilient, adaptive, and dependable. These mutually dependent qualities are essential for intentional competence. Resilient individuals apply healthy coping skills and stress management strategies to navigate the VUCA reality. They have the energy and optimism necessary to endure crises. Adaptive individuals are emotionally intelligent leaders who approach novelty with a sense of optimism and curiosity to learn and grow. They are receptive to feedback and always willing to challenge the status quo. Individuals and leaders are dependable when they are both credible and reliable to do what they say and say what they do.

Leaders facilitate intentional competence across the team through a combination of coaching, teaching, and mentoring specific to the development and growth needs of the individual. We will discuss the CTM Methodology later, but for now, leaders need to know how to push their people, when to push them, and how hard to push them to expand and deepen their level of competence and confidence so that they are comfortable in otherwise uncomfortable situations.

At the organizational level, intentional competence is integrated into the foundation of how the organization does business. It describes an environment that encourages development, learning, and innovation; provides stretch opportunities; and establishes a framework for effective and timely decision making.[67] Let's explore these qualities in more detail so you can develop intentional competence for your organization:

Encourage Development: Organizations must invest in their people. They make it easy to attend education and training programs as a core function of the job. Leadership makes every effort to accommodate participation in programs for both professional and personal development. Because people are the mission, these programs are a priority. That means the organization is not only willing to foot the bill but also willing to allow employees to complete training and attend classes during the standard workday. Leaders play an active role through counseling and evaluations to ensure employees are going to school, attending seminars, and seeking professional accreditations to further their development.

Encourage Learning: Organizations must create a psychologically safe environment where people are allowed to fail. Employees cannot be afraid to make mistakes. Failure is seen as a learning opportunity, and organizations have constructive ways to learn from mistakes. One example for how to do this is through the after action review (AAR). The AAR is more than an assessment. It helps teams understand what happened as opposed to what was supposed to happen, why it happened, and what team members can do differently in the future to improve results. The organization captures best practices and lessons learned for the next iteration in a judgement and blame free environment. The template the army uses for the AAR, which takes place after every mission, is included in Figure 11.

AFTER ACTION REVIEW

This template applies in both formal and informal settings for activities ranging from routine training events to major combat operations and everything in between.

Step 1. What was supposed to happen?

- Examine how the plan was developed and communicated
- Understand how the solution was meant to achieve the desired end state
- Review any standards of performance or measures of effectiveness

Step 2. What actually happened (organizational level)?

- Gather the facts including key events, major milestones, contingencies, achievements, or any other fact relevant to the organization's understanding of the problem and implementation of the solution
- Gather perspectives from different stakeholders about what happened in an objective, non-judgmental way
- Evaluate how well the organization achieved the standards of performance or measures of effectiveness

Step 3. Assess what happened (operational level)

- Be candid in describing what went right and wrong with what happened
- Consider how the organization defined the problem, developed potential solutions, and implemented those solutions
- Invite all stakeholders to participate and provide feedback from their perspective. Each stakeholder should provide their own assessment about what went well and areas of improvement

Step 4. Determine the way forward

- Invite each member of the team to identify areas to sustain and improve during the next opportunity
- Establish accountability and a schedule for implementing any changes or improvements

Although not always feasible, it can help to have an outside observer provide oversight to collect information, provide feedback, and present findings for review.

Figure 11. The Army's Template for the After Action Review.[68]

Encourage Innovation: Leaders empower others to try new things and take calculated risks. The VUCA state of play is one where an effective solution today might not be effective tomorrow, and those closest to the action have the best perspective to address emerging challenges quickly and effectively. When leaders encourage innovation, anyone can challenge the status quo regardless of role, position, or job function. Leaders seek input and constructive feedback from people with diverse backgrounds, experiences, and perspectives. The goal is not ownership or credit but continuous improvement to maintain momentum and adaptability in an ever-changing environment.

Encourage Growth Opportunities: Leaders provide stretch opportunities to condition developing leaders to be more comfortable in uncomfortable situations. A stretch opportunity is one that goes just beyond the threshold of an employee's resume in terms of education, training, or experience. It can be directed toward an individual or the entire team to increase awareness and expose potential blind spots. Stretch opportunities are the equivalent of throwing a beginning swimmer into the deep end of the pool in a controlled environment to see how well they can swim. It's better for an employee to struggle and make mistakes under your supervision than it is for them to struggle and flail around when they're out on their own. Providing stretch opportunities increases an individual's confidence and poise to operate in otherwise uncomfortable situations.

Establish a Collaborative Decision Making Framework - This framework combines intuition and logic for timely and effective decision making. Leaders have the courage and confidence to follow their gut but allow and even encourage others to challenge the logic of their reasoning. They don't make decisions in a box, and they understand how to filter out the noise to focus on what's important. Leaders acknowledge the limitations of their assumptions and biases, and they recognize that the person in charge doesn't necessarily have the best ideas. Consequently, these leaders surround themselves with experts and smarter people for a respectful discourse. Active participation in this process achieves a learning effect for everyone involved that increases an organization's ability to make timely and effective decisions in the VUCA reality.

After integrating the above strategies, you will have developed the habits of an organization postured to grow and adapt in times of ambiguity and uncertainty. Your employees and teams will evolve to meet unexpected or unanticipated challenges. When combined with the mutual trust that comes from alignment to shared values and common purpose, you'll have the foundation necessary to be agile in the VUCA reality.

Communicating Vision with the **Statement of Intent**

Leaders must be able to communicate their vision in a way that is easily understood and remembered by everyone in the organization. Employees can't be expected to deliver if they don't know what success looks like. Building off the foundation of mutual trust and intentional competence, the next level in the Hierarchy of Organizational Agility is providing a statement of intent to describe the leader's vision for success.

A statement of intent is a clear and concise expression of the activities and the desired end state to provide focus and help each department, business unit, and function achieve the intended results without any further instruction - even when circumstances unfold in unexpected ways.[69] If you were to envision a continuum of management oversight and control with micromanagement on one end and full-autonomy on the other, the statement of intent is as close as the organization can get to full-autonomy while still functioning as a team. This is why a leader's intent is so important for organizational agility. A statement of intent empowers employees to act in the absence of definitive guidance or approval to do so.

The three elements to the statement of intent come from the military version of the commander's intent and include *purpose, key tasks,* and *end state* (see Figure 12). The purpose is *the WHY* describing how the particular course of action aligns with the broader purpose and mission of the organization. It connects the leader's vision to the bigger picture. Key tasks are *the HOW* outlining the critical activities and objectives that must be completed to achieve the desired outcome. What makes a task "key" is its significance to the overall effort. They provide the path to the desired outcome. Failure to complete a key task means failure in your mission.

STATEMENT OF INTENT	DETAILED DESCRIPTION
PURPOSE Set the foundation	Answers the question WHY and connects to the larger purpose of the organization
METHOD • Publish the book to provide the core reference and marketing material • Market the program across the public, private, and nonprofit sector to increase awareness and build the value chain for service delivery • Deliver workshops to validate the program of leadership development • Develop a certified training program to build a professional faculty	• The key tasks (no more than 6) that the organization **must accomplish** • Written as a task (WHAT you will do) with a purpose (WHY you are doing it): <u>Task:</u> Deliver online workshops <u>Purpose:</u> To validate the program of leadership development
END STATE Internal Standard: Formalized partnerships with individuals and organizations in the public, private, and nonprofit space External Standard: (1) Coaching program validation, (2) B Corp Designation, (3) Government Registration as a Woman Owned Minority Business Functional Standard: Complete 3 Leadership Development Workshops	The definition of success broken down into three components: Internal Standard: How we see ourselves External Standard: A credible standard of how the rest of the world sees us. Functional Standard: Acceptable Business Metrics

Figure 12. Example of Statement of Intent with Detailed Description of the Purpose, Method, and End State.

End state defines *WHAT* winning looks like. It is the desired outcome for the organization. In the military, end state is typically described in terms of friendly forces (see yourself), enemy forces (see the enemy), and the terrain (see the environment). A nonmilitary application wouldn't describe success by these terms. Therefore, an analogous framework includes an *internal, functional,* and *external* standard of success.

Let's explore the *internal standard* first. This is a measure of the tangible and intangible qualities of the team when the mission is done. Conditions that shape this internal perspective might include metrics from restructuring initiatives, changes to the labor force, management turnover, surveys about the culture or leadership climate, employee resilience and commitment, human resources activities, individual training and development, or the status of facilities. The internal standard describes what winning looks like from inside the organization.

The *functional standard* represents the business case for success. For some organizations, that could be revenue, profit and loss, market share, stock price, production output, etc. For other organizations - such as a nonprofit, success and failure could be based on the number of clients, the level of social change, the passage of new laws, or the introduction of new policy. The functional standard should be familiar to you. It's how you would normally assess success or failure.

Finally, the *external standard* represents an objective measure of success from an outsider's perspective. It describes the relationship between the organization and the legal, social, cultural, and economic factors of the environment. It might include consumer ratings and reviews, standards of industry performance, awards and recognition, credentialing, compliance reports, community engagement, or the public narrative. The challenge is to define this standard with verifiable facts. In doing so, you build a reputation and brand from multiple stakeholders across your business ecosystem.

Military units must succeed in all three areas (friendly, enemy, and terrain) to achieve a complete victory. The same is true for the internal, external, and functional standards in the nonmilitary application. There are more than a few examples (including fraud and hostile workplaces) to validate that true winning requires more than the straight dollars and cents of success. Organizations can collapse from an unethical culture (internal standard). The organization's reputation could suffer irreparable damage from a loss in consumer confidence (external standard). Profitability is only one measure of success. **Victory in the VUCA reality requires leaders achieve a comprehensive end state regarding how they see themselves, how they perform in their industry, and what their relationship is with society as a whole.**

A general rule to consider when crafting a statement of intent is that less is more. The goal is to empower - not control. Therefore, the statement of intent should be no more than a single paragraph: One sentence for the purpose (WHY), four to five sentences for the method (HOW), and three sentences for the end state (WHAT). It should be written in a language every employee can quickly read, understand, and easily remember. Once approved, it is shared across the entire workforce. Think of the statement of intent as giving your team permission to be creative and innovative within certain boundaries, allowing everyone across the organization to seize upon opportunities as they arise.

Process Optimization in Dynamic Operations

Once the vision is set, the next step for the leader, like a coach, is to mobilize subordinate divisions, staff functions, and business entities to develop a coordinated plan of action to achieve the desired end state. This is where the rubber meets the road. The military uses a highly adaptable operations process to develop, communicate, and optimize plans for coordinated action with decentralized execution. This is a dynamic process for developing sound solutions in complex or evolving environments. We translated this process for nonmilitary use. It's called the CADEnce Method (Coordinated Action for Decentralized Execution). We will briefly describe this process here and go into greater detail in the next chapter.

The CADEnce Method empowers organizations and their teams by giving them a step-by-step methodology to plan, prepare, execute, and assess solutions to problems. The CADEnce Method is a form of process optimization because it combines inputs from multiple perspectives building a shared understanding. It enables timely decision making so leaders can direct action as the situation warrants. Business functions become a collaborative force enhancing organizational agility by cutting through the bureaucracy and stovepipes that inhibit progress. The CADEnce method is a living construct that shapes how your team thinks so that they can evolve with the conditions of their environment.

Disciplined Initiative and Risk Acceptance

Agility is achieved when employees have the confidence, competence, and commitment to act without formal guidance or permission to do so. This requires a combination of disciplined initiative from employees and risk acceptance from leaders. These are complementary actions that together can achieve organizational agility in the VUCA environment.

The nature of the VUCA reality suggests opportunities present themselves in very unpredictable and unanticipated ways. Changing situations and new information can render a plan useless. This happens when you don't control all the factors or stakeholders in the environment. Employees are *disciplined* because any action they take is informed by your statement of intent. The key tasks and end state provide the guiding framework. Based on the urgency of the situation, employees are entrusted, encouraged, and expected to take the initiative to move the organization closer to the intended outcome.

Employees must understand that any action taken is not in isolation. Although implementation is decentralized, employees are still part of a larger team and working toward a common goal. When taking initiative, your team must be mindful of how their actions align with the broader intent and whether the benefit of said action outweighs the potential cost of desynchronizing the rest of the team.[70]

Initiative requires confidence and courage. The will to act outside formal instructions or guidance isn't easy. The alternative is to wait for permission and approval, wasting valuable time. The cost to the organization is a potential opportunity lost. Taking action requires a level of comfort with the uncomfortable responsibility to act without complete information. Effective decisions combine the urgency of the situation with the best information available in a position to influence the outcome in a positive way.

The pressure of this moment looms large for junior leaders. This is the leadership moment. It is an unenviable position to feel the weight of the situation reduced into a single moment. All eyes are on you. The entire point of the ADAPT Framework is to prepare leaders with the confidence, competence, and commitment to lean into these moments - especially the ones that occur outside the purview of executive control. This is why the statement of intent is so important. It provides just enough guidance to take action at the decisive moment to achieve the desired outcome. This is how organizations become more agile.

Agility offers you the decision space to act by your own volition. When you have the initiative, you can respond in a way that controls how a situation might unfold. You can shape events to your strengths. You can shield your vulnerabilities. You can be decisive and dictate how and when events unfold. If you don't have the initiative, that means someone else does, and you become reactive. You surrender your ability to control the outcome. It's hard to imagine winning under those constraints. This is why disciplined initiative is so important in the VUCA reality. By empowering everyone across the organization, you increase the depth of opportunities to take and retain the initiative as conditions unfold to achieve your desired outcome.

Empowering your team comes with some risk. Your team needs to know that you have their backs. In agile organizations, leaders accept the consequences of the team's actions - good, bad, or ugly. This is why mutual trust and intentional competence provide the foundation for organizational agility, and it is also the nature of leadership in the VUCA reality. Employees need to feel safe because YOU accept the risk. We covered this in the GTG Leadership Approach. When things work out, the employees receive the credit, but when things don't, the leader accepts the consequences. The leader stands accountable for everything the organization does or fails to do.

Just as employees may feel uncomfortable with the responsibility to act when the situation dictates, it is natural for leaders to feel uncomfortable with the risk they incur in this environment. The level of trust and control you offer the rest of your team should be at the limit of your comfort level, and sometimes, one step beyond that threshold. Always look to manage and mitigate risk, but don't be paralyzed by it. This is the burden of leadership, and why the sequence of activities forms a hierarchy of behaviors for organizational agility. Being risk averse and waiting for the perfect scenario could achieve the opposite effect and close the window of opportunity.[71]

To manage uncertainty, leaders consider the impact of possible hazards to the plan and continuously seek strategies to mitigate those hazards. They provide guidance by outlining those key tasks the organization must do, but they leave enough latitude for employees to exercise their creativity and innovation. Leaders set decision points to modify or change a course of action as circumstances evolve. Regardless of the speedbumps, they continue moving forward. They set the example with their confidence, competence, and commitment moving the organization forward through uncomfortable spaces.

The story about the casualty evacuation in the beginning of this chapter is an example of disciplined initiative to achieve the broader intent. Because we were grounded in our shared values, accepting that risk was nothing more than doing the right thing. We were expanding MEDEVAC to reduce the casualties in Afghanistan, and we had enough knowledge of the area of operations to apply our best judgment to mitigate hazards and achieve the mission. We did it without approval. We did it without the requisite coordination. We did it to save a life. If we had run into trouble, we were hours away from any support, but the risk of not taking action outweighed the risk of doing the mission. That's the nature of agility. There is risk in taking the initiative, but if you exercise sound judgment and trust your team to do the same, there is nothing stopping you from capitalizing on opportunities to succeed in the VUCA reality.

Apply the Hierarchy of Organizational Agility Concept Summary

The nature of the VUCA environment requires organizations to have a high level of agility in order to capitalize on opportunities to achieve desired results. Adapting the military construct of mission command into the Hierarchy of Organizational Agility provides a means to attain agility as an organizational state of being. In this hierarchy, organizations must have a foundation of mutual trust and intentional competence. Intentional competence describes an organization's priority for personal and professional growth through learning. Leaders build off that foundation by describing a clear and concise vision of what success looks like. This statement of intent connects the organization's activities to a larger purpose, outlines a method with key tasks to meet the objectives, and provides a comprehensive description of what success looks like. This statement of intent becomes the guiding framework for members of the organization to act when an opportunity presents itself.

Across the organization, the staff functions and business units come together to develop creative solutions that continuously evolve in a dynamic environment. They become coordinated yet decentralized in their actions to achieve the intent, and they provide relevant information for timely decision making. Each level in the Hierarchy of Organizational Agility builds upon the previous level to set the conditions for every employee to be empowered with the right information to make the best decision and take appropriate action when the situation warrants. In this state of dynamic operations, leaders continuously manage and accept risk - providing the guidance and support as the entire team strives forward toward the intended outcome. Through dynamic operations, the organization has the agility to anticipate change, shape conditions to create an advantage, and seize opportunities to win in the VUCA reality.

Considerations to Apply the Hierarchy of Organizational Agility

The following questions provide a method to assess strengths and potential areas of growth to achieving an agile state of being in the VUCA reality:

- How does your organization achieve intentional competence by encouraging learning, development, and innovation?

- How does your organization provide employees with stretch opportunities and establish a framework for proactive decision making?

- How does your leadership describe and communicate a comprehensive vision of success that everyone knows and understands across the organization?

- How does your organization empower individuals and teams to take action in the absence of specific guidance or permission to do so?

- How do leaders manage and accept risk in trusting the judgment of junior leaders and employees to take the initiative?

8 | PROCESS OPTIMIZATION FOR FINDING SOLUTIONS

I think it's very important to have a feedback loop, where you're constantly thinking about what you've done and how you could be doing it better.

- Elon Musk

Change is fast and often unexpected in the VUCA environment, so how do you keep everyone on the same page and moving in the same direction? How do you encourage initiative and stay synchronized toward a common objective? How do you streamline communication so that the right information gets to the right person at the right time to make the best decision? In this chapter, we will discuss an effective, cyclical process to plan, prepare, execute, and assess operations in the modern VUCA reality.

The army combines art and science in a very structured, detailed approach for solving complex problems that military leaders can expect in combat. They call it the operations process, and this methodology is taught, trained, and evaluated with consistent frequency and repetition throughout the entirety of a leader's military career. The operations process is so prevalent throughout the military culture that it becomes integrated into a leader's subconscious and informs their intuition for understanding and solving problems. Army leaders apply this approach to everything they do including both regular training events and complex combat operations alike. Applying the operations process is one of the most formative habits of the military leadership experience.

In writing this book, our challenge was to condense and translate the meaningful pieces of the operations process into a single chapter that you and your organization can apply to develop actionable solutions in the modern VUCA reality. We call this nonmilitary model of process optimization the CADEnce Method. Coordinated action and decentralized execution describes the state of play for dynamic operations. The CADEnce Method synchronizes the planning effort to empower business functions, staff elements, and subordinate teams to operate efficiently, effectively, and independently while working toward a common goal. It optimizes processes to get everyone on the same page and moving in the same direction. The objective is to get ahead of the game and place your team in a position to win.

Introduction to the CADEnce Method

Consulting firms like the Boston Consulting Group describe the challenge of creating successful business ecosystems (a living network of organizations and stakeholders to deliver a product or service) as one that must continuously evolve. While adaptability provides a competitive edge, the ecosystem design requires a solid plan of action as the foundation. Successful ecosystems must also leave room for creativity, serendipitous discoveries, and flexibility for emerging customer needs. Ecosystems that hope to succeed over the long run must be ready to modify their design in anticipation of shifts in markets, technologies, regulations, and public sentiment.[72]

But let's be honest, failures in organizational strategy and transformation don't occur in the design but in the implementation. It's the preponderance of weak links in the framework that become exposed vulnerabilities during execution. Some of the weak links might include:[73]

- Unclear values and conflicting priorities
- Poor coordination
- Inadequate leader development
- Inadequate vertical communication

Building a malleable and living ecosystem for your organization can be achieved using the CADEnce Method. *CADE* is short for *C*oordinated *A*ction, *D*ecentralized *E*xecution. The word "cadence" means rhythm. As an adaptation of the operations process, the CADEnce Method allows your organization to establish a rhythm - or what the army calls a "battle" rhythm - of activities to plan, manage operations, and make timely decisions in a dynamic environment. This is how organizations get into the flow when facing a challenge in the modern VUCA reality.

The CADEnce method integrates each of the steps we've covered in the ADAPT Framework. As a leader using this method, you can expect your team to:

- Create a common operating picture and shared understanding of the situation.
- Consider divergent and creative ideas.
- Set priorities, identify constraints, challenge assumptions, provide a way to track progress, and establish accountability.
- Create a feedback loop incorporating lessons learned.
- Recognize risks and blind spots.
- Optimize time available.
- Streamline communications to determine who needs to know what and when to facilitate timely decision making.
- Provide meaningful options that address the core issue or problem
- Set the conditions to capitalize on opportunities when they arise.
- Synchronize actions across teams and business functions for decentralized execution toward a common goal.

The CADEnce Method (see Figure 13) includes six basic steps: situation analysis, collaboration, solution development, communication, solution implementation, and assessment and adjustment. It is a living process with the flexibility to adjust and modify solutions as necessary to achieve the intended outcome. Once completing the final step - assessment and adjustment - the process returns to situation analysis and repeats itself until you reach your goals. The beauty of the CADEnce Method is that it also creates a learning environment for members of your team. Your role as a leader is twofold: (1) To provide direction and motivation, and (2) To coach, teach, and mentor as appropriate to the situation.

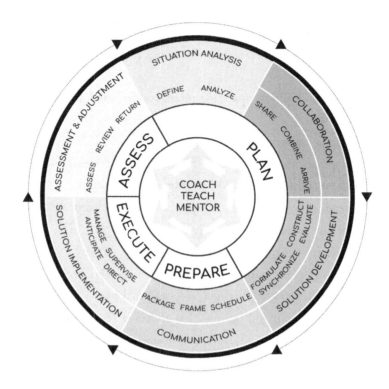

Figure 13. Process Optimization: The CADEnce Method

In the military, the operations process is a collaborative activity involving the entire staff. By incorporating all staff functions, commanders develop a comprehensive picture of the situation, problem, and potential solutions. Likewise, the CADEnce Method mobilizes analogous business functions and activities. A functional comparison between the military staff elements and the equivalent, nonmilitary business functions is included in Figure 14. In addition to staff elements, organizations should consider including major business units. The objective is to create an inclusive process that accounts for all perspectives.

MILITARY STAFF		NONMILITARY EXECUTIVE STAFF EQUIVALENTS
TITLE	FUNCTION	TITLE (CHIEF, VICE PRESIDENT, DIRECTOR, SENIOR MANAGER)
S1	Personnel Officer	Human Resources, Diversity, Workforce Management
S2	Intelligence	Marketing, Business Development
S3	Operations and Training	Operations (and derivatives of operations), Sales, Learning, Training, Leadership, Compliance
S4	Logistics	Logistics, Supply Chain Management, Facilities, Engineering
S5	Plans	Strategy, Research, Innovation, Business Continuity, Business Development
S6	Signal	Information and/or Technology
S7	Financial Management	Finance, Investment, Revenue
S8	Civil Affairs	Public Relations, Social Media
S9	Chief of Protection	Security, General Counsel, Risk

Figure 14. Comparison between Military Staff and Nonmilitary Staff Equivalents

It is important to note that the CADEnce Method is just a model. There is an art to how it is applied. How you execute this model depends on a variety of factors including the experience of your team, the time available, and how long everyone has been working together. You can abbreviate or extend this process based on your understanding of the situation and the intended outcomes. More time might be necessary based on the level of ambiguity or complexity. All of these considerations influence who participates in the planning effort. To get a better understanding of the CADEnce Method, let's explore each of the six steps in greater detail.

CADEnce Method STEP 1: Situation Analysis (Planning Stage)

The situation analysis in this model is analogous to the mission analysis from the military decision making process. This is typically the most challenging and time intensive step. Based on the leader's vision and statement of intent, each person on the planning team independently defines the problem and identifies all the relevant information that could impact potential solutions. A description of the inputs, activities, and outputs from this process is included in Figure 15.

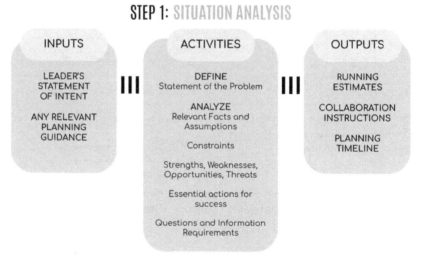

Figure 15. Situation Analysis Inputs, Activities, and Outputs

Situation Analysis Inputs

Understanding the vision must precede any analysis. Leaders describe that vision through the statement of intent. Leaders supplement that vision with initial guidance for the planning effort based on their understanding of the situation and experience. Armed with the intent and initial guidance, each member of the planning team conducts their own, independent analysis by function, department, and business unit. Be as inclusive as possible to increase the depth of the analysis. Your objective is to paint a picture of the situation from multiple perspectives.

98

Situation Analysis Activities

Situation analysis requires the team to define the problem. A problem statement is a concise description of the gap between where the organization is and where it wants to be based on your intent. Your challenge here is to **distinguish the root cause of the problem from the symptoms of the problem.**[74] Addressing the symptoms won't necessarily get you where you want to be. For example, a drop in revenue might only be a symptom of a deeper problem in the organization or strategy. It is important to clearly define and articulate the problem so - as conditions change - you can assess whether or not the nature of the problem has changed. Addressing the "wrong" problem can create complications or take the planning team down rabbit holes. Investing time on the front end to accurately define the problem saves time and frustration as you begin to implement solutions on the back end.

Once you've defined the problem, it's time to analyze it. Analysis includes identifying relevant facts and assumptions, constraints, SWOT (strengths, weaknesses, opportunities, and threats), essential actions for success, and your questions and initial information requirements. Let's examine each of these elements in greater detail.

Relevant Facts and Assumptions. A fact is a known, verifiable and relevant truth about the situation. An assumption is information accepted as true in the absence of facts but cannot be verified.[75] **Facts are preferred over assumptions. The number of assumptions should be based on facts and limited to those necessary to continue the planning process.** Never make assumptions based on other assumptions. You elevate the risk of failure when you base a plan on information that is only presumed to be true. Leaders at all levels should track the assumptions to confirm or deny their validity as circumstances evolve and new information becomes available.

Constraints. A constraint is a restriction that reduces your team's ability to take action.[76] Constraints typically consume time, money, resources, or a combination of the three. Constraints dictate both what an organization can do and what it cannot do. Some examples of constraints might include credentialing or licensing, compliance and statutory requirements, or limitations incurred due to restrictions like a hiring freeze. Constraints prescribe the obligations and boundaries for the planning process.

Strengths, Weaknesses, Opportunities, and Threats (SWOT) Analysis. Be aware and brutally honest about your team's strengths and weaknesses. A strong sense of camaraderie or experience could be a strength, and the lack of those qualities could be a weakness. Furthermore, identify potential opportunities and vulnerabilities that may either accelerate or hinder progress. This independent analysis by business function shapes the narrative about how each member of your team supports the big picture. The SWOT also establishes a baseline to identify potential risks to the plan or operation.

Essential Actions for Success. Each team member identifies the critical actions they must accomplish in order for the organization to achieve the intended outcome. They utilize their expertise and experience within their respective lane to recognize the critical milestones essential to the success of the overall organization.

Questions and Information Requirements. Recognizing the gaps in the available information as well as any unanswered questions are critical to the planning process. Analysis is based on known information, but it is equally important to acknowledge the known unknowns and the questions that might reveal "unknown" unknowns. Shared understanding in this environment means answering or at least acknowledging all of the known and unknown factors that influence the problem.

Situation Analysis Outputs

The key outputs from the situation analysis include the running estimates, instructions for collaboration, and the planning timeline.

Each staff element or business function defines and analyzes the problem from their particular point of view. Once they paint an initial picture, they have a responsibility to track changes and update their analysis on a routine basis or as the circumstances evolve. The document that tracks those changes and information updates is called the **running estimate.**

The running estimate is a continuous assessment of the situation used to determine if ongoing activities are proceeding in a manner to achieve the desired outcome.[77] The format for running estimates is based on organizational preference but should include those data points critical to ensuring that the organization remains on glide path. Running estimates are living documents. They allow your team to quickly review progress and address necessary changes. At a minimum, EACH business function and subordinate business unit should maintain a running estimate that includes relevant facts and assumptions, constraints, a SWOT analysis, essential actions for success, open questions, and information requirements. Tracking new information and changing conditions is imperative to problem solving and decision making in the VUCA reality, and the running estimate is a proven tool to navigate this challenge.

Collaboration instructions provide the entire team guidance for integrating their analysis into a shared understanding of the situation. The detail and depth of this guidance is based on the experience and expertise of the team and the time available. Think of the planning effort in terms of project management. These instructions would include the designation of a project manager to supervise the planning team and overall planning effort. In larger organizations - and in the military - the executive officer or chief of staff fills this role. These instructions might include who needs to participate in the process and how it should unfold. Choose the right person who can be accountable for the entire planning effort.

Finally, the **detailed planning timeline** should outline milestones, scheduled meetings, and expected deliverables. Consider crafting this timeline jointly with the members of the planning team. Set expectations early. Your team shouldn't have to guess what's required of them. A best practice from the military is a technique called backward planning. This is where you start with the desired time for execution (solution implementation) and work backwards to the present. Populate the timeline with the necessary milestones, scheduled meetings, and deliverables. This provides structure in an otherwise fluid environment. More importantly, it allows your team to manage time and resources in a proactive way.

As the foundation for the planning effort, the situation analysis is the most important step in the CADEnce Method. It alerts and mobilizes the planning team, orients or redirects the organization toward the intended outcome, and establishes an inclusive framework for creative problem solving. The first step of this planning effort provides an independent snapshot of the situation from multiple perspectives. From these different points of reference, you can monitor, modify, and direct action as new information becomes available or the nature of the problem changes.

CADEnce Method STEP 2: Collaboration (Planning Stage)

The objective of Step 2 of the CADEnce Method is to combine the independent analyses from Step 1 to create a shared understanding of the situation. You achieve this through **collaboration**. This step begins with building the organizational perspective of the situation that includes relevant factors, the most probable and most dangerous scenarios, potential opportunities, information gaps, and ends with a comprehensive definition of the problem. A description of the inputs, activities, and outputs from this process is included in Figure 16.

STEP 2: COLLABORATION

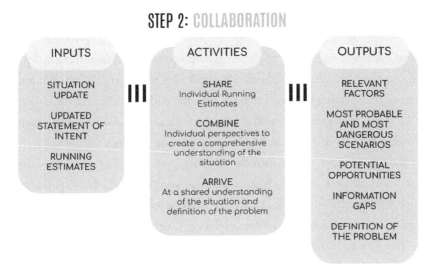

Figure 16. Collaboration Inputs, Activities, and Outputs

Collaboration represents the first of three meetings through the CADEnce Method. When it comes to conducting any meeting in the VUCA environment, preparation is important. Set an agenda that outlines the discussion topics, time allotted for each topic, and desired outcomes. Identify and communicate who should attend, when and where the meeting will take place, what information will be presented, and any other special instructions. Effective meeting management focuses the team on deliverables. Efficiency is key. Build routines of best practices to optimize productivity while minimizing the time requirement.

Collaboration Inputs

The collaboration inputs include a situation update, an updated statement of intent, and each business function's running estimate of the situation. Don't overlook the situation update. Change is the only constant in the VUCA reality. It is not uncommon for conditions to change in the time it took to define and analyze the problem. Include an azimuth check at the beginning of each meeting to ensure the team is working with the most updated information and any related changes to the statement of intent.

The chief of staff or planning project manager is responsible for the administration and execution of the collaboration session - as well as every other meeting in the CADEnce Method. This includes managing the agenda and the conduct of the meeting to keep the team on time and on target. At the conclusion of the meeting, they publish detailed minutes with results and hold team members accountable for any due outs and post-meeting requirements.

Each team member comes into the meeting prepared to present their running estimate and answer questions about their analysis. Set the conditions for inclusive, meaningful dialogue. Ensure the right people are in the room. You want a meaningful discussion. Therefore, collaboration should be a priority for key leaders from every business function across the organization.

Collaboration Activities

This meeting includes individual presentations that showcase each business function's running estimate, potential issues, and open questions. Presenters should be prepared to answer questions from the audience. A best practice is to select an individual from the planning team to record and track relevant information, themes, and questions that arise from the presentations. Your objective is to paint a common operating picture of where you are as an organization and where you want to go.

After the presentations, the real work begins. Shared understanding requires an appreciation for different perspectives and interrelationships between business functions. No business function exists in isolation. For example, the time it takes to recruit and train a sales staff may impact the marketing strategy and launch of a new product line. This may require coordination between human resources, training and development, business development, marketing, finance, and operations. Collaboration allows each stakeholder in the plan to see and understand the entire ecosystem of functions and operations.

Encourage inclusive, open dialogue with a curious mindset. You want people to challenge the assumptions and the status quo. Invite dissenting points of view. Don't start solving the problem at this point. Collaboration is a framing activity.

It requires divergent thinking to achieve a comprehensive understanding of the problem. Keep an open mind and put everything on the table. Give yourself and the team the best chance to identify the core issue standing in the way of your objectives.

Collaboration Outputs

The collaboration meeting should identify the following:

Relevant Factors. Identify what is meaningful to the entire organization. Distill the information from the independent analyses to recognize what is important to the organization as a whole. This part of the analysis helps the entire team understand the context of the problem from an organizational perspective. This understanding can inform the statement of intent and concept of the operation. Relevant factors underpin the logic connecting the vision to actionable solutions.

Most Probable and Worst-Case Scenarios. Envision the most likely way events will unfold based on what you know. Recognize potential threats and pitfalls. This allows you to account for risks in a proactive way. In doing so, you create a competitive advantage. By recognizing the hazards, you can identify mitigation strategies to continue moving forward. You stay ahead of the game by anticipating scenarios and shaping future events.

By considering the worst-case scenario, you can anticipate those actions necessary to rebound and regain momentum when setbacks occur. By accounting for the possibility of failure, you get a leg up in responding to the environment instead of reacting to it. The moment you become reactive, you surrender initiative, momentum, and control over the outcome. Retain decision space even when things aren't going as expected. Understanding the most likely and worst-case scenarios sets the conditions to continue moving forward even when setbacks occur.

Potential Opportunities. In addition to recognizing the hazards, you want to identify potential opportunities. You can even anticipate and shape conditions to create opportunities. Opportunities come from competitive advantages based on your strengths and understanding of the situation. You can identify opportunities by functional area or collectively as an organization. Exploring opportunities is an optimistic approach based on what you can do as opposed to what you cannot do.

Information Gaps. Expect information gaps. This is the VUCA reality. You won't know everything. Some questions may not have answers. That's okay. The key is to see where these gaps exist in a collaborative forum. Work to fill the gaps by assigning responsibility to different members of the team to find answers. Provide a deadline and a way for sharing answers across the group (group folder, digital platform, formal presentation, email, etc.). This keeps everyone involved, alert, aware, and accountable in the planning process.

Problem Statement. Defining the problem is the most important outcome from collaboration. The problem statement describes where the organization is and where it wants to be based on the statement of intent. Think of the problem statement as a grounding rod. In the VUCA reality, the nature of the problem can change quickly. The problem statement ensures everyone is on the same page and sets the stage for developing coordinated solutions.

The individual in charge of the planning process (chief of staff or planning project manager) is responsible for collecting outputs and providing the in-progress review. This may take the form of a presentation for senior leaders or decision makers. The format depends on the complexity of the analysis, experience of the staff, and personal preference. Group presentations are preferable when numerous open issues are identified so that the entire organization can contribute and benefit from the discussion.

Consider how you can leverage collaboration to coach, teach, and mentor junior leaders. Increase your capability for subsequent iterations or future planning efforts. Teach your team how to think through the problem by doing it in real time. This develops future leaders, and it also helps subordinates understand how you think, process information, and make decisions. By understanding "what the boss wants," your team can anticipate, prepare, and act in the absence of direct guidance.

Use collaboration as an opportunity to provide bottom-up refinement of the intent. This is where the science of the process informs the art. Examine and refine the method (key tasks) and definition of success (end state) based on the analysis. Provide guidance for any open issues and look for possible decision points. Provide direction for the planning effort that accounts for the urgency of the problem and the capabilities of the team. Once you've processed and understand the analysis, you are ready to move to Step 3 of the CADEnce Method.

CADEnce Method STEP 3: Solution Development (Planning Stage)

Solution development is the culmination of the planning effort. This is where you generate options to achieve the end state. Based on the leader's guidance, the planning team may develop a single option or multiple courses of action. The decision to plan one or more options depends on the time available, your shared understanding of the problem, the experience of the team, and the organization's familiarity with the problem. A description of the inputs, activities, and outputs for Solution Development is included in Figure 17.

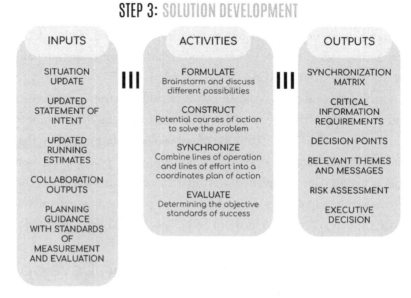

Figure 17. Solution Development Inputs, Activities, and Outputs

Solution Development Inputs

To begin the planning process, you'll need an update of the situation, the outputs from the collaboration meeting, any modifications to the statement of intent - as appropriate, and planning guidance that includes metrics for success. Once you've gathered the tools, the chief of staff or planning project manager can update the planning timeline, and the team can come together for the second of three meetings in the CADEnce Method.

Planning guidance is critical for solution development to focus the team in the time available. Include how you intend to measure progress and the level of success. Building a plan without standards for evaluation is like playing basketball without knowing the rules or how to keep score. Standards for measurement and evaluation set the parameters for identifying acceptable solutions (screening criteria), evaluating potential solutions (evaluation criteria), and measuring progress toward the intended objective (measures of performance and measures of effectiveness). These metrics determine how to keep score and recognize whether you are winning or losing.

Screening criteria establish the parameters for an acceptable solution to the problem.[77] These standards require planners to answer several critical questions:[78]

- Suitability: Does the solution actually address the core problem in a legal and ethical way that is consistent with our values?
- Feasibility: Do we have the resources available for this solution?
- Acceptability: Is the benefit of the solution worth the cost or risk incurred?
- Distinguishability: How does this solution differ from other possible options or what we've done in the past?
- Completeness: Does this solution address the problem from beginning to end?

Screening criteria are the go/no-go standards for any plan of action.

Evaluation criteria allow you to measure progress and assess the likelihood of success.[79] The best way to explain evaluation criteria is through some examples (see Figure 18).

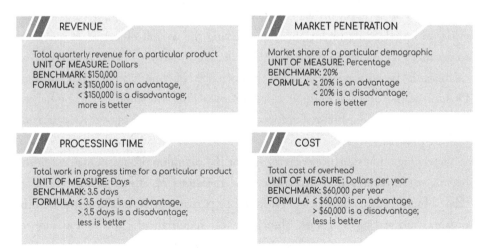

Figure 18. Evaluation Criteria Examples

Generally speaking, evaluation criteria include a title, definition, unit of measurement, a benchmark, and a formula to assess desirability.[80] The quantitative nature of the criteria increases the objectivity of your analysis. Notice how the evaluation is measured against a standard - or benchmark. If you have multiple options, don't compare them against one another at this point. Evaluate each option on its own merits. Pay attention to interrelationships and be discriminating with your evaluation criteria. You want to avoid having two criteria that end up measuring the same thing.

Keep biases to a minimum. Capture the underlying factors for success, and let those factors inform your evaluation criteria. Developing evaluation criteria in advance of the planning effort helps prevent groupthink and **confirmation bias,** the tendency to search for, interpret, favor, and recall information in a way that confirms or supports one's prior beliefs or values. It is not uncommon for planners to get passionate about their ideas. That passion can obscure objectivity. Work to remove any bias in your evaluation criteria.

Not all criteria are created equal. Some may be more important than others. How you weigh criteria depends on the level of detail you want from this analysis. You can score criteria on a graduated scale or assign a weight to a particular criterion based on its importance to achieving the overall objective. If you want to get more technical, you can even use a decision matrix to perform a numerical calculation based on the relative importance of one criterion to another. Document the process you use to keep score. This information can be helpful during the assessment phase to understand flaws or shortcomings in your decision making process.

Screening and evaluation criteria are for the planning process. Once execution begins, use **measures of performance** and **measures of effectiveness.** These are related but separate constructs. A measure of performance describes how well the organization executes a task, function, or requirement, and a measure of effectiveness assesses the associated change - positive or negative - as it relates to progress toward the desired objective.[81] Every action should have a task (a thing you do) and a purpose (why you do it). The measure of performance describes how well you do the task, and the measure of effectiveness describes how much closer - or further - you are from your desired result. In other words, the measure of effectiveness lets us know whether or not the tasks we perform are actually achieving the intended effect.

For example, let's say that your organization sets an objective to increase revenue by 10 percent in the next fiscal year. In order to achieve that goal, the organization plans on increasing sales calls by 30 percent. The measure of performance tracks the total number of calls you make. When you achieve a 30 percent increase, you have met the standard, but remember, the goal is to increase revenue. This is where the measure of effectiveness comes into play. It answers the question of whether or not revenue actually went up 10 percent. The task was to make more calls, but the purpose of that task was to increase revenue. Using measures of performance and measures of effectiveness show the cause and effect for a more critical analysis of your strategy and actions.

Throughout the planning process, designate tasks and activities for business functions to accomplish. For each activity, your team should identify a measure of effectiveness (the purpose or WHY) and a measure of performance (the task or WHAT). This allows subordinate managers and employees across the organization to assess and understand the nature and effectiveness of their actions. For anything your organization does in the VUCA reality, every employee should know WHAT they are doing and WHY they are doing it. This knowledge informs decision making during decentralized execution.

Solution Development Activities

Once you've gathered the tools, planning can begin. Your primary goal is to be creative, inclusive, and objective, while developing actionable solutions within the given time constraints. Guided facilitation is crucial to formulate, construct, synchronize, and evaluate possible solutions.

Leaders **formulate** plans through brainstorming and divergent thinking. Based on your shared understanding of the problem, the chief of staff or planning project manager facilitates open and curious dialogue about possible solutions.

Independent thinking while guarding against premature analysis is key. At this point, you want creative ideas - the more, the better.

Once the brainstorming process begins to lose momentum, combine related ideas into coherent options for further consideration. There is no set number of options needed for further analysis, but more options will take more time. In some situations, leaders may prescribe a particular solution or provide specific guidance for the number of options the team should analyze. Every option you generate must pass the screening criteria before planning can continue.

In the next phase of solution development, **construct** a written concept of the operation. This is called a solution statement. This is an executive summary of the plan. A solution statement can be as short as a sentence or as long as a paragraph depending on the nature of the problem. The solution statement describes the key and essential actions necessary to achieve the end state.

Once you have a general concept, it's time to get into the details. You do this by mapping out that concept in space and time. Start from the end state and work backwards. Identify the incremental benchmarks and milestones by function or business activity necessary to achieve the definition of success. Each one of these benchmarks should have a measure of performance and measure of effectiveness. Everyone across the team should consider how their specific function or expertise contributes to each benchmark and milestone.

These activities form the basis for the *lines of operations* and *lines of effort*. A line of operation is a logical sequence of activities for a specific business unit. For example, a line of operation for hiring might include recruiting, screening applications, interviewing, making an offer, and onboarding. A line of effort is a cross functional sequence of activities to achieve milestones and objectives from the statement of intent.[82] A line of effort captures the interrelatedness of organizational activities to achieve group outcomes. A particular plan might include several lines of operation and lines of effort.

Let's look at an example. Consider a situation where a healthcare facility is looking to add a new clinic. Clinic expansion would be the line of effort, and activities like hiring new staff and providers, marketing outreach to increase awareness, quality control and accreditation, and logistics for equipment and supply would be the supporting lines of operation. A project manager typically oversees the cross functional effort, while leaders and managers within business functions oversee particular lines of operation. Applying this methodology allows you to visualize how complicated operations unfold in time and space.

Building off this example, let's say that this healthcare facility is looking to expand services to include urgent care. This would be another line of effort that would involve multiple lines of operation. Over the course of a year, it is not uncommon for a business to have several lines of effort. Breaking down cross-functional activities using lines of operations and lines of effort helps your team understand the logic of how each piece of the business fits into the bigger picture of how the organization will get to where it wants to go.

Each line of effort is essential to accomplish the mission, and the next step in the planning process is to **synchronize** the lines of operation and lines of effort into a single, coherent plan. If you've ever worked in an organization where it felt like everyone had their own agenda, chances are that leaders never synchronized their efforts. You only have so many people and so many resources, and synchronization allows the team to allocate those resources based on priorities and constraints to both integrate and optimize business functions toward a common goal.

Begin with the end in mind. Identify the crucial lines of effort necessary to achieve the end state. Work backwards to capture the conditions and milestones necessary to meet the overall objective of the line of effort. By the time you arrive back to the present day, you've created a comprehensive list of conditions and specific tasks that map out a path to the end state. Do each line of effort independently before overlaying the activities for all lines of effort. Once you overlay these activities, you may notice some conflicts. You might also notice coordination requirements between business functions. This is an expected and desirable outcome of the process. Remember, you are all on the same team, so you don't want to be competing for limited resources. The objective is to integrate efforts toward a common goal.

Once you've integrated the lines of effort into a coherent plan, walk through it chronologically to see if it makes sense. This allows you and the entire team to foresee potential problems, decisions, and contingencies.[83] The army calls this wargaming. Wargaming is nothing more than a disciplined process to visualize the flow of events. Think of it as a type of rehearsal. The most common technique for the wargame is the action, reaction, and counteraction method. In other words, you or another external agency (competitor, government, environment, population, customer base, etc.) initiates an action that elicits a reaction from customers, competitors, or the environment. Based on that reaction, planners consider the appropriate or likely counteraction for the situation.

In order to optimize this process, establish a red team to act as a devil's advocate. This can be one person or a group of people who challenge planners on how circumstances might unfold. The red team combines the threats and weaknesses from the SWOT analysis with the assumptions underpinning the plan to play out the most likely and most dangerous scenarios. No action in the VUCA reality comes without consequences, and the red team helps planners understand the second and third order effects of their actions. This synchronization technique pushes planners to question the logic of the solution and uncover any blind spots. It disciplines the process from the pitfalls that come from anchoring, confirmation bias, and groupthink.

Let's look at the example of the same startup consulting firm we referenced earlier when we outlined the statement of intent in Figure 12. The graphic in Figure 19 illustrates the lines of effort, lines of operation, key objectives, and decision points for the fiscal year. In this example, there are two lines of effort - *program development* and *partnerships*. Within the line of effort for program development, there are three lines of operation: *book, workshop,* and *credential.* Within the *partnership* line of effort, there are also three lines of operation: *public, nonprofit,* and *private.* The key objectives are in rectangular boxes. These key objectives should relate to the statement of intent. Decision points are indicated by the numbered stars.

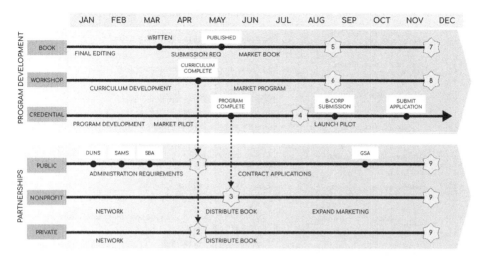

Figure 19. Lines of Effort and Lines of Operation Including Key Objectives and Anticipated Decision Points

This graphic shows the interrelatedness between multiple lines of effort in a single, coherent plan. Notice how the objectives in the *program development* line of effort relate to decision points in the *partnerships* line of effort. Because this illustrates the organization's annual business plan, decision points occur later in the year. This should be expected in the VUCA environment. Each of the decision points is related to critical information requirements (see Figure 20). Remember, a decision point just signals a time in space where you would make a decision. You can choose to do nothing, or you can even delay a decision. The point of this graphic is to understand how events might transpire to anticipate any potential setbacks.

DECISION POINT	CRITICAL INFORMATION REQUIREMENT IF CONDITION	THEN DECISION or ACTION
1	System Award Management (SAM.gov) registration approved	Begin soliciting contracting opportunities
2	Curriculum Development Complete	Begin soliciting private partnerships B2B
3	Coach Certification Program Complete	Begin Nonprofit partner solicitations
4	5 Faculty participants for pilot program	1. Update website to meet credentialing requirements 2. Begin 3 month virtual training program
5	Book sales exceed 100 units per month or designated best seller	1. Create audible version 2. Explore speaking engagements
6	Workshop sales 2 or more simultaneous or 3 total clients	1. Expand workforce for program delivery 2. Develop Asynchronous Content
7	Book sales less than 10 units per month	1. Expand Direct Marketing & Outreach (Podcasts, Interviews, etc.) 2. Rewrite and/or relaunch
8	No workshop sales	1. Seek funding for marketing 2. Create partnered programs 3. Diversify market (government, academic, B2C)
9	Status of Partnerships	1. Expand number of partners 2. Focus partnership in one line of operation 3. Introduce B2C marketing

Figure 20. Relationship between a Critical Information Requirement (CIR) and a Decision Point in the IF-THEN format

Operating in the VUCA environment is a lot like playing chess. You want to visualize your opponent's moves before they happen. It is important to recognize and monitor the indicators and signals for potential problems or challenges. Recognize the factors and conditions that will drive future decisions. The information feeding into this process includes the critical information requirements and decision points. By anticipating future events, you can shape them into an advantage that allows you to retain initiative and momentum. These are critical qualities to retain in the VUCA environment.

You might have multiple plans or courses of action to consider. If so, repeat this process to synchronize each option. Once you've mapped out all the potential plans, you are ready to **evaluate** them. The evaluation process identifies the course of action that will:[84]

- Pose minimum risk to the organization and the desired outcome
- Posture the organization for future success
- Empower employees to exercise disciplined initiative
- Optimize flexibility and decision space for unexpected threats and opportunities
- Create a unified communications strategy and messaging

As a reminder, options should not be compared against one another but against an objective standard of success using the evaluation criteria. The goal is to recognize the strengths and weaknesses of each course of action and select the option with the greatest probability of success. Consider the advantages and disadvantages of each course of action. When combined with a quantitative assessment tool like a decision matrix, this process combines intuition and analysis for a comprehensive understanding of the strengths and weaknesses of each option under consideration.

In its entirety, solution development harnesses the knowledge, creativity, experience, and diversity of your team to critically analyze and develop sound, logical solutions to a problem. This process applies the science to balance the art from the leader's intuition to inform decision making and solution implementation in the VUCA reality.

Solution Development Outputs

Solution development is the most tedious step in the CADEnce Method. It also delivers the most detailed outputs. Solution development outputs include the synchronization matrix, critical information requirements, decision points, relevant themes and messages, and the risk assessment.

The **synchronization matrix** is the resultant product from the staff walking through the plan while considering the most likely and most dangerous scenarios. The typical format is a detailed list of activities in chronological order. It highlights the key actions and cross-functional coordination in time and space to meet the benchmarks and milestones.

Critical information requirements (CIR) represent the required information to make timely decisions as events unfold. What distinguishes information as *critical* is the situation-dependent, time-sensitive nature of that information for a decision that directly influences the desired outcome.[85] The CIRs determine reporting and information sharing guidelines for the communication step in the CADEnce Method.

A **decision point** is a specific point in time and space where executive leaders anticipate making decisions. A decision point does not dictate what the decision must be, only when and where it should be made to optimize capabilities or reduce vulnerabilities. Decision points acknowledge the incomplete nature of information in the VUCA reality but also signal when conditions will require direct action. At a minimum, a decision point should outline the nature of the decision, who is responsible for making the decision (if required), and the CIRs that inform the decision (see Figure 20 for an example of the relationship between CIRs and decision points).

Relevant themes and messages define the broader internal and external communication strategy for coherent messaging across the organization. These are essential to align marketing campaigns, business development, customer interactions, and media engagements. These may include talking points, narratives, or press releases to ensure everyone across the organization is speaking with one voice.

Throughout the synchronization process, the team is continuously performing **risk management** within their functional area. "Risk management is the process of identifying, assessing, and controlling risks arising from operational factors and making decisions that balance risk cost with mission benefit."[86] The process of risk management involves the following five steps:[87]

STEP 1: Identify the Hazards. These are the problems, obstacles, and dangers that could result in mission failure.

STEP 2: Assess the Hazards. Your team should consider the probability (extremely likely, likely, random, unlikely, extremely unlikely) that the hazard will occur and the severity (extremely high, high, moderate, low, negligible) of the hazard in terms of how it impacts your potential to achieve the intent.[88]

STEP 3: <u>Develop Controls</u>. A control is an action or decision that reduces the probability or severity of the hazard. Control measures should be integrated into the synchronization matrix for each solution.

STEP 4: <u>Implement Controls</u>. This step establishes accountability for the controls. Implementing controls identifies how a control measure will be executed and who is responsible for supervising that execution.

STEP 5: <u>Supervise and Evaluate.</u> The initial risk assessment is just a starting point. Risks may change as circumstances evolve, causing your mitigation strategy to change. Therefore, it is important to actively supervise, evaluate, and adjust your assessment and control measures throughout planning and execution.

Uncertainty and ambiguity can paralyze an organization. This five-step process for risk management acknowledges the hazards without impeding progress toward the desired end state.

The final step of solution development is when the team recommends a plan for a decision. This recommendation typically takes the form of a presentation. As a part of this presentation, the team should include all facts and assumptions relevant to the problem, a discussion of the options, analysis-based conclusions, and any coordination necessary to execute.[89] The team can also offer guidance based on what they have learned about the problem, coordination requirements, CIRs, decision points, messaging, and risk.

This step concludes when the plan is approved for implementation. Don't allow the desire for perfection to be your enemy. An 80 percent solution might more than suffice given the nature and uncertainty of the problem. If there is no decision, the team goes back to the drawing board. This happens when conditions change or new information fills some pre-existing gaps. Be conscious of the time available. Delays to retool the plan could limit your flexibility and decision space during execution. Once you have approval of the plan, shift your focus to preparation for execution.

CADEnce Method STEP 4: Communication (Preparation Stage)

In fluid environments, communication is a major factor for success. Communication is about how you manage and share information. Everyone needs to know the plan. Knowledge and transparency with relevant and timely information empowers employees at all levels to take action when opportunities arise.

Information management facilitates efficiency and impactful decision making. On the one hand, incomplete or inaccurate information could cripple the organization from poor decisions. On the other hand, the inability to filter information (i.e. "Does the boss need to know?") could overwhelm decision makers with meaningless data and superfluous information. This step in the CADEnce Method optimizes how you manage and share information. The inputs, activities, and outputs for the communication step are included in Figure 21.

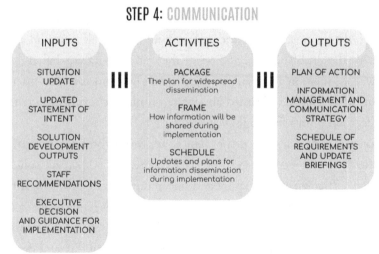

STEP 4: COMMUNICATION

INPUTS	ACTIVITIES	OUTPUTS
SITUATION UPDATE	PACKAGE The plan for widespread dissemination	PLAN OF ACTION
UPDATED STATEMENT OF INTENT	FRAME How information will be shared during implementation	INFORMATION MANAGEMENT AND COMMUNICATION STRATEGY
SOLUTION DEVELOPMENT OUTPUTS	SCHEDULE Updates and plans for information dissemination during implementation	SCHEDULE OF REQUIREMENTS AND UPDATE BRIEFINGS
STAFF RECOMMENDATIONS		
EXECUTIVE DECISION AND GUIDANCE FOR IMPLEMENTATION		

Figure 21. Communication Inputs, Activities, and Outputs

Communication Inputs

As with every step in the CADEnce Method, start with the situation update, an updated statement of intent (if necessary), and the planning products from the previous step. Include any bottom-up recommendations from the team on how to package, frame, and schedule updates during execution. Finally, ensure you have a clear understanding of any constraints for sharing information across the team.

Before you disseminate the plan, ensure everyone involved in the planning process is on the same page. One technique to validate everyone's understanding is the **brief back**. A brief back is where the person receiving the instructions, guidance, or presentation verbally reflects their understanding of the plan. This is how you verify that the message received matches the message sent. Everyone inside the huddle of the planning effort should understand the plan before you start sharing it with the rest of the organization. If the people who developed the plan aren't on the same page, there is little chance that the people outside the huddle will have a shared understanding of the plan.

Communication Activities

Be mindful and deliberate with how you share information across the organization. Promote greater efficiency and effectiveness through how you package, frame, and schedule communications.

Package. In the military, information is packaged in a document called the operations order - or OPORD for short. This is an involved process. The conventional OPORD consists of five paragraphs - situation, mission, execution, sustainment, and command and control. In addition to the base order, subordinate and special staff publish appendices with instructions and guidance specific to their functional area. For large, complex operations, the base order and appendices could span hundreds of pages.

The OPORD facilitates parallel planning across multiple echelons. Most civilian organizations are not as stratified as military units, so packaging can be reduced and simplified for nonmilitary applications. **There is a delicate balance between substance and simplicity.** Include enough detail so people understand the overall plan and their responsibilities without wasting their time sifting through pages and pages of minutiae to find out what those responsibilities are. Your objective is to empower - not encumber - business functions and employees across the organization.

In order to save time, build a template that streamlines requirements. This is the core purpose of standardizing the OPORD format in the military. One example of what this might look like is included in **Figure 22: The Solution Implementation Guidance and Instructions (SIGI)**. This particular template recalibrates the five-paragraph military order into a more simplified, appropriate, and manageable framework for nonmilitary applications.

Date/Number: Identify a date time group and numerical designation to differentiate one plan from another. This tracks the most current information and instructions.

PART 1: OVERVIEW OF THE PROBLEM

1. **Problem Statement:** The definition of the problem
2. **Relevant Facts and Assumptions:** This enables a deeper understanding across the organization to recognize when the facts and planning assumptions have changed
3. **Most likely and most dangerous scenarios:** This helps employees to recognize the necessary indicators for proactive decision making.

PART 2: OVERVIEW OF THE SOLUTION

1. **Statement of Intent:** Purpose, Method, and End State
2. **Concept:** The statement or paragraph that concisely explains the solution to the problem.
3. **Subordinate tasks by function.** Each task should include a measure of performance and measure of effectiveness. To increase understanding, it is helpful to create an execution matrix that details the sequence of events across the organization in real time. The staff can create this from the Synchronization Matrix.
4. **Critical Information Requirements:** This alerts all employees to the information and data required for executive decision making. The CIR should follow this general format:

- The specific details of the information and who is best postured to provide that information
- Who (senior managers, executive leaders, etc.) needs to be alerted of this information
- When the notification should occur (immediately, within 24 hours, etc.)
- How the information should be shared (email distribution, phone call, in-person, etc.)
- Any immediate actions necessary at the point of action (typically the person making the report) in order to take advantage of an opportunity or mitigate a vulnerability

5. **Decision Points:** Decision points should highlight the following:

- When the conditions warrant an executive level decision
- Who is the person expected to make a decision
- How the rest of the organization will be informed about the decision
- What are the potential follow-on actions such as branches or sequels to the existing plan

6. **Relevant Themes and Messages:** These are the talking points and themes of any advertising, marketing, or publicity campaigns.
7. **Risk Assessment:** The planning team includes the risk assessment so everyone is aware of the potential hazards and the necessary control measures to mitigate those hazards.

PART 3: BUSINESS ADMINISTRATION AND RESOURCE MANAGEMENT

1. **Business Administration:** Any special instructions regarding a specific organizational functions such as human resources, finance, compliance, or other routine/scheduled activities that might be impacted through solution implementation
2. **Resource Management:** Any special instruction that involve supply, inventory, transportation, facilities, or budgetary guidance during solution implementation

PART 4. COMMUNICATIONS

1. **Framework:** How information will be shared throughout solution implementation.
2. **Schedule:** Timeline and suspenses for reporting include, method, format, and means of delivery.

Figure 22. The Solution Implementation Guidance and Instructions (SIGI) Template

This checklist captures relevant information, guidance, and instructions to execute a particular course of action. Consider this example a starting point and customize this template to meet the needs of your organization.

Frame. Set standards for communication. More specifically, determine *what* information needs to be shared, *who* needs it and *when, how* it is shared, and *where* someone can go to find it. Start with the CIRs and decision points - the information essential for you to direct and manage execution. The standard for critical communications is normally immediate, and the means for communication is typically a direct conversation. The standard for what constitutes a CIR should be high. Not everything is a priority. You don't need to know everything right away. Trust that your people will handle their responsibilities and let you know when they run into a problem.

The military has proven techniques to efficiently and effectively manage how information is shared. These instructions would be included in Part 4 of the SIGI. Here are a few examples:

Optimize digital platforms. Create a digital library with shared folders and locations for specific information, data, and reports.

Use Bottom Line Up Front (BLUF) reporting. Many army units use templates for serious incident reporting (SIR). The format includes the 5 W's - Who, What, Where, When, and Why. Leaders preparing the message would add context by adding two more W's - "What you are currently doing about it," and "What assistance is required - if any." This provides an executive summary of critical events.

Adopt "screenshot" email messaging formats. This approach optimizes email message traffic. As a forcing function, it requires the author of an email to limit their text to 21 lines in standard font to ensure that the recipient can read the entire message on their screen (hence the name "screenshot") without scrolling.

Employ quad charts for routine reporting. A "quad chart" is a single slide broken down into four quadrants - one for each topic. In the military, those topics included a statement about what happened (last day, week, or month), what is expected to happen (next day, week, or month), what significant accomplishments or setbacks occurred, and what assistance (resources, time, and clarification) is necessary. Quad charts standardize the routine reporting format for cross-functional teams.

Outline communication procedures. Not everything requires a phone call or the boss's attention. Filter what information is shared, how it is shared, and when it is shared. Use all the forms of information management at your disposal - text, chat, email, shared folders, message boards, etc. Keep the phone lines open for critical communications.

Build habits for information management. You do this by creating standing operating procedures, the policies that dictate how an organization accomplishes routine business. This sounds like a lot now, but once you have the templates created and expectations set, your entire team will be able to efficiently and effectively manage large volumes of information. More importantly, you will retain organizational bandwidth to handle emergent and unforeseen issues.

Schedule. *When* you share information is included in the schedule. **Set expectations and establish predictability.** In combat, most military units conduct a daily update briefing that covers what happened the last 24 hours, what is expected to occur over the next 24 hours, and any significant events, resource constraints, or other issues that require the commander's attention. This is normally when the staff and subordinate units brief their quad charts. When not deployed to combat, these briefings occur weekly or bimonthly. The frequency is determined by the nature of the operations. The military calls this schedule of activities a *battle rhythm*. The battle rhythm establishes a sustainable cadence of activities so that leaders and employees alike can manage their time.

Be disciplined to the point of being draconian with meeting management. Every meeting should have an objective, an agenda, and deliverables. Keep meetings brief. Don't hold meetings just to share information. Keep them action oriented toward specific objectives. If there is nothing significant to cover, guidance to disseminate, or decisions to be made - cancel the meeting. Time is the one resource you can't get back. More time spent in meetings means less time spent working toward objectives. As a general rule, no person should spend more than 5 percent of their time in group meetings (not to be confused with counseling, coaching, mentoring, or other one-on-one engagements). This means that for a 40-hour work week, spend no more than two hours in group meetings. That's an ambitious goal to say the least. *Spending more time in meetings could indicate a lack of priorities, unknown or unclear expectations, no internal procedures for communication, the absence of a clear vision, indecisiveness, lack of trust, or an unwillingness to collaborate.* Optimize the meetings you have to maximize the time available to achieve your objectives.

Communication Outputs

The most important deliverable from this step is a simple, yet detailed plan of action for widespread dissemination to the entire organization. As a part of the plan, include the details of your communication strategy (what, who, how, and where) and the instructions for information management - reporting formats, briefing slides, email templates, shared file access and directories, and any other guidance to streamline information sharing. Finally, publish a schedule of meetings, in-progress reviews, and reporting requirements. Set conditions to manage information and communicate effectively so that you can handle unforeseen challenges as they arise.

CADEnce Method STEP 5: Solution Implementation (Execution)

Solution implementation marks the changeover from preparation to execution. This is when the plan goes into motion. The inputs, activities, outputs for solution implementation are included in Figure 23.

STEP 5: SOLUTION IMPLEMENTATION

INPUTS	ACTIVITIES	OUTPUTS
SITUATION UPDATE PLAN OF ACTION INFORMATION MANAGEMENT AND COMMUNICATION STRATEGY SCHEDULE OF REQUIREMENTS AND UPDATE BRIEFINGS	MANAGE Priorities, resources, and risk SUPERVISE At the most vulnerable point of failure in the plan ANTICIPATE Outcomes, shape them to your advantage, and respond to consequences DIRECT Decisions and actions to seize opportunities and maintain the initiative	MEASURABLE PROGRESS TOWARD THE INTENDED OUTCOME AND DESIRED END STATE

Figure 23. Solution Implementation Inputs, Activities, and Outputs

Solution Implementation Inputs

Publishing a plan isn't enough. Everyone needs to understand it. Provide ample time for your organization to digest the information and ask questions. Preserve time for employees to conduct their own planning and preparation. As a point of reference, the army uses the ⅓ - ⅔ rule. This means that planners take one-third of the time available to develop and brief the plan and the remaining two-thirds of time remaining is left for subordinate planning and preparation. Use brief backs and spot checks throughout the organization to validate understanding. **Decentralized execution requires an employee's thorough understanding of their responsibilities.**

Solution Implementation Activities

Execution is the focus of solution implementation. Expect deviations to occur as conditions evolve. As a leader, your job is to manage, supervise, anticipate, and direct actions to achieve the objectives.

Leaders **manage** priorities, resources, and risk. They don't micromanage others. Know what is most important for your team to achieve success. Your priorities are determined by the **center of gravity** - the decisive factor that tips the scales

127

toward success or failure. Align information requirements and decision points to manage risk and sequence actions to balance opportunities and vulnerabilities. **Don't get lost in the weeds.** Maintain your perspective of key objectives and milestones.

Supervise at the time and place of the most vulnerable or opportune moment. Put yourself in a position to influence the most critical point of the operation. Provide oversight when and where the risks are greatest. Ask probing questions. When in charge, focus on the big rocks. Empower others to take care of everything else.

Effective leaders **anticipate**. They stay one step ahead of events as they unfold. Keep one eye in the present, and one eye looking forward. Don't ruminate about the past - even if you make a poor decision. When mistakes happen, address the issue promptly and let it go. You can't change what has already occurred, so don't waste your time or energy. Focus on moving forward. Consider the actions you can take now to shape conditions to your advantage in the future.

Direct action based on the situation. When things are going well, maintain momentum. When things aren't going well, seek opportunities to regain the initiative. Be decisive - especially in the leadership moment. You won't always have perfect information. Make the best decision possible with what's available. Consider the risks, weigh the costs and benefits, and then take action. Yes, this will be uncomfortable, but that is the nature of leadership.

Solution Implementation Outputs

Military commanders are mindful of two timeless lessons when beginning any operation: (1) *The best laid plan never survives first contact with the enemy,* and (2) *Fight the enemy - not the plan.* The first lesson means that things won't always go as expected. In combat, the enemy gets a vote, and they don't always behave in a manner that suits your plan. The second is based on the first, and it serves as a reminder that plans only offer a basic framework. Focus on the statement of intent to achieve your objectives.

128

In a nonmilitary context, concentrate your efforts on what you control. Even when everything seems out of control, use measures of performance and measures of effectiveness to monitor your progress toward the desired outcomes. Track your CIRs and decision points to stay one step ahead of problems or contingencies. Consistently revisit the facts and assumptions underpinning the plan. Leverage expertise across the team and encourage others to challenge your logic. Build a sustainable routine to protect against burnout while meeting the demands of the situation. Remember, leadership moments happen when you least expect them, so stay vigilant!

CADEnce Method STEP 6: Assessment & Adjustment (Assess Stage)

The final step in the CADEnce method is assessment and adjustment. This is the final of three meetings in the CADEnce Method. Assessment includes an evaluation of external factors, internal factors, and progress toward the intended outcome. This is your comprehensive review of how the team is doing. If things are going well, understand what worked to maintain momentum. If things are going poorly, recognize what is not working and make the necessary adjustments to get back on track. The inputs, activities, and outputs from the Assessment & Adjustment Step are included in Figure 24.

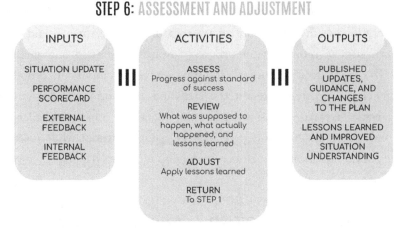

Figure 24. Assessment and Adjustment Inputs, Activities, and Outputs

Assessment & Adjustment Inputs

In order to conduct an objective assessment, you need the most current update of the situation, all quantitative metrics, and any qualitative feedback. The **situation update** is the first and most important part of your assessment. You should be used to this requirement by now! Stick to the facts. See the situation as it really is and not how you might want it to be. Combine quantitative metrics with qualitative analysis to paint the most accurate picture of what is happening.

Your **performance scorecard** comes from the measures of performance and effectiveness. It is a quantitative assessment based on known facts. Use real time data to conduct an objective assessment of your benchmarks and milestones. Data is important, but data alone is not enough.

The qualitative analysis comes from **external** and **internal feedback**. External feedback comes from customers, partners, and other entities outside the organization. Internal feedback comes from within the team. Collect feedback through surveys, questionnaires, assessments, or direct conversations. In many cases, the qualitative analysis can predict a positive or negative shift in the quantitative metrics. Stay connected to the people. Keep your finger on the pulse to understand what is really happening across the organization on a deeper level.

Assessment & Adjustment Activities

Identify assessment requirements during the solution development phase that includes a schedule of in-progress reviews. Scheduling can be based on time (weekly, quarterly, annually) or by event (benchmark, milestone, or end state). The specific activities for this step include assess, review, adjust, and return.

Assess. Use the measures of performance, measures of effectiveness, CIRs, external and internal feedback, and intermediate milestones to assess your team's performance and progress toward the intended outcomes. What is the data telling you? Put the pieces together to obtain the clearest picture of what is happening. Solicit competing perspectives and divergent points of view. Including different interpretations minimizes bias and provides the most comprehensive picture of what is really going on.

Review. The assessment tells you *what* happened, and the review helps you understand *how* and *why*. Look for correlations or causal relationships. Walk through the steps of the AAR (see Figure 11) to review what happened, how it happened, and why events unfolded the way they did. Confirm or deny the underlying foundation for the plan by acknowledging how ongoing activities and new information impacts your original analysis of the situation (facts, assumptions, constraints, SWOT, open issues, etc.). Be open to the idea that the nature of the problem may evolve over time.

Adjust. Any adjustments require a delicate balance between patience and courage. You need patience to stay the course when you experience setbacks provided that the framework of the plan is still valid. You need courage to change course when the current path is no longer tenable, or the nature of the problem has changed. Receiving critical information, reaching a decision point, or experiencing an unexpected change in circumstances may require an immediate adjustment. Trust your intuition. It is not uncommon for leaders to call an audible based on their experience and understanding of the situation. Any such adjustments should be limited in duration and scope. These are immediate actions you take based on the urgency of the situation. Address more deliberate or complex changes when you return to Step I of the CADEnce Method.

Return. The final step of this process completes the cycle. The CADEnce Method concludes when the end state is achieved, or the current operations are no longer tenable. Just like when you started this process, set a timeline for planning and review moving forward. Address two fundamental questions as you begin the next iteration: (I) Are we solving the right problem, and (2) Are we making progress toward the solution? The answers to those basic questions shape what happens in the next round of planning.

Assessment & Adjustment Outputs

The outputs from this step are broken down into immediate actions and future planning efforts. Immediate actions are just that - actions the organization must take to capitalize on an opportunity or mitigate a vulnerability. Future planning efforts require the following:

- Updated statement of intent (as necessary)
- Results of the AAR
- Lessons learned
- New information bearing on the problem
- Other guidance as appropriate for the next round of planning

Once you've produced the outputs, you are ready to return to STEP I: Situation Analysis. In doing so, you don't necessarily have to start from scratch. Because you've already done extensive analysis, keep what's relevant and scrap the rest. Abbreviate and even skip steps as appropriate. For example, you may already have a solid communication strategy with effective standards of performance. If that's the case, don't revisit these subroutines. Make deliberate changes grounded in your understanding of the problem and analysis of the solution.

The first time you execute this process for a new initiative, operation, or program will likely be the longest and the most involved. For subsequent iterations, address specific challenges and continue moving forward towards the end state. That's how this process works. Integrate the CADEnce Method into the cognitive framework of how your organization does business. Develop routines for managing the typical planning, collaboration, communication, execution, and assessment products. Create the standing operating procedures to guide those routines. Develop habits for an inclusive, creative, and sound process for finding solutions to complex problems.

Mastery of this process takes time and practice - a lot of it! Be patient. If this is your first time using the CADEnce Method, start small. Begin with a statement of intent and build your running estimates by functional area. From there, establish the templates for meetings, communication, and information management. Work through the steps at a pace you can handle. If possible, leverage the expertise from a veteran leader in your organization with experience in design methodology and the military decision making process. Through frequency and repetition, find efficiencies and make this process your own.

The CADEnce Method is more than just a step-by-step process to find solutions. It is a way of thinking through problems in situations where you don't have all the information and conditions are always changing. It is a cognitive approach to function effectively in dynamic environments. Over time, these activities become second nature. More competence in the process feeds your confidence to develop solutions to complex challenges. With a combination of competence and confidence, your team can commit to achieving the end state.

Process: The CADEnce Method Summary

The CADEnce Method is a dynamic hub that brings together all the spokes of your organization's business functions so you can turn the wheel of progress. Situation analysis, collaboration, solution development, communication, solution implementation, and assessment and adjustment describe the cycle of activities to enhance efficiency, transparency, and collaboration. By integrating the entire team into the process, you encourage critical analysis and innovation. By integrating this approach in how your organization does business, you can refine the problem solving process during routine activities to build your resilience for more unpredictable times. The CADEnce Method provides a template to hone your ability to solve the most complex problems.

Success in the VUCA reality requires leaders to be comfortable in extremely uncomfortable situations. This is a learned skill and one of the most important qualities of leadership in today's uncertain world. You can't do everything yourself. Empower employees at the very limit of your comfort range - and then take one step beyond that. Commitment works both ways. The team trusts you to lead. Trust their competence and confidence to do their job. If they lack competence or confidence, then you have some work to do now - before the next crisis.

This is where the other aspects of the ADAPT Framework prepares you for the challenges of solving complex problems in the VUCA reality. We align individual values and purpose to create a common character as a foundation to guide actions and behaviors. This is so we can place trust in our people. We develop a culture of camaraderie so that members of the team can depend on each other to deliver their best effort. This is so that the people can place trust in each other. We apply the Hierarchy of Organizational Agility so that individuals have the competence and confidence to take the initiative. This is so that people can learn how to trust themselves. Set conditions now for leaders across the organization to be as comfortable as possible with the uncomfortable nature of the VUCA reality.

Process: Considerations for Coordinated Action with Decentralized Execution in the VUCA Reality

The following questions provide a method to assess strengths and potential areas of growth for solving complex problems in ambiguous and uncertain environment in an inclusive and collaborative way:

- How does your organization facilitate an inclusive and creative dialogue to define and analyze complex problems?

- How efficient and effective are your processes for collaboration?

- How does your organization synchronize activities across different initiatives, business units, and programs to coordinate actions and define priorities?

- What guidelines does your team follow to manage information and direct communication so that leaders have what they need when they need it to make decisions?

- How does your organization capture and apply lessons learned to adapt to changing conditions in an incremental or dynamic way?

9 | TRANSFORM LEADER ENGAGEMENT

A leader is like a shepherd. He stays behind the flock, letting the most nimble go out ahead, whereupon the others follow, not realizing that all along they are being directed from behind.

-   Nelson Mandela

Make people your mission. That's how you win in today's uncertain world. Better people make better employees and better teams in the face of adversity. If you want people to become better versions of themselves with the competence, confidence, and commitment to achieve any mission then transform leader engagement through the CTM Methodology. Coaching, teaching, and mentoring facilitate personal growth and improve performance providing the foundation for effective leader behaviors in high performance organizations.

Many organizations hire professional coaches, pay top dollar for executive education, and adopt formalized programs for mentorship. In other words, they outsource solutions for personal growth and professional development. This is where the military is different. They don't outsource solutions. In the military, your boss serves as the primary coach, teacher, and mentor to facilitate guided discovery learning for personal growth and professional development. Their job is to raise individual and collective competence, confidence, and commitment to the limit of their potential. Military leaders commit to building better people. In doing so, they make better service members. In the context of applied psychology, this approach is called *transformational leadership*.

Overview of Transformational Leadership

The Full Range Leadership Model was developed by Bruce Avolio and Bernard Bass, two renowned psychologists and experts in the field of organizational behavior. According to their theory, leader behaviors function along a continuum beginning with a hands-off approach on one end, progressing through transactional forms of management, and arriving at transformational leadership as the most engaged approach at the other end.[90] Since developing this theory in the 1990s, there has been overwhelming empirical evidence to validate the correlation between transformational leadership behaviors and improved organizational outcomes.[91] Consequently, transformational leadership has emerged as one of the most popular and most studied models of contemporary leadership theory.

Transformational leadership addresses the limitations of more transactional forms of management. Management distributes power and incentives through extrinsic rewards and punishments - if you do *this*, then you will get *that*. Transactional forms of leadership and management use carrots and sticks. Unfortunately, this approach marginalizes the intrinsic drive that every employee brings into an organization.[92] This intrinsic drive fuels creativity, perseverance, confidence, and determination to achieve one's full potential. Harnessing that motivation to inspire performance requires something more than management. It requires leadership.

Transformational leadership describes the behaviors necessary to optimize individual performance to achieve organizational results. The four competencies of transformational leadership include: idealized influence, inspirational motivation, intellectual stimulation, and individualized consideration - often referred to as the "Four-I's".[93] A description of the activities for transformational leadership and how they apply to the CTM Methodology is included in Figure 25.[94]

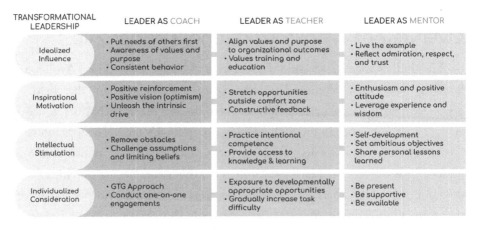

TRANSFORMATIONAL LEADERSHIP	LEADER AS COACH	LEADER AS TEACHER	LEADER AS MENTOR
Idealized Influence	• Put needs of others first • Awareness of values and purpose • Consistent behavior	• Align values and purpose to organizational outcomes • Values training and education	• Live the example • Reflect admiration, respect, and trust
Inspirational Motivation	• Positive reinforcement • Positive vision (optimism) • Unleash the intrinsic drive	• Stretch opportunities outside comfort zone • Constructive feedback	• Enthusiasm and positive attitude • Leverage experience and wisdom
Intellectual Stimulation	• Remove obstacles • Challenge assumptions and limiting beliefs	• Practice intentional competence • Provide access to knowledge & learning	• Self-development • Set ambitious objectives • Share personal lessons learned
Individualized Consideration	• GTG Approach • Conduct one-on-one engagements	• Exposure to developmentally appropriate opportunities • Gradually increase task difficulty	• Be present • Be supportive • Be available

Figure 25. Coach, Teach, and Mentor Methodology: the Four I's of Transformational Leadership applied to the ADAPT Framework

138

Transformational leadership works in elite military units, and it is the behavioral model that best describes the leader engagement in the ADAPT Framework. It aligns individual values and purpose with common values and a shared vision while fueling the motivation to ascend the hierarchy of needs toward self-actualization.[95] Transformational leaders are also visionaries who are team-centric, engaging, inspiring, inclusive, emotionally intelligent, and collaborative.[96] Transformational leaders cope with change by providing a new vision, aligning people to the vision, and inspiring people to achieve that vision.[97] People come first in transformational leadership.

The Coach, Teach, and Mentor (CTM) Methodology

As shown in Figure 25, coaching, teaching, and mentoring are mutually supportive activities that align with the Four I's of Transformational Leadership. The CTM Methodology is the nonmilitary application of *guided discovery learning* - an advanced form of engagement that optimizes learning by integrating new circumstances with an individual's personal base of knowledge and experience.[98] Coaching facilitates discovery. Teaching enables learning. Mentoring provides guidance. The CTM Methodology allows leaders to adjust their style or method of engagement to create moments of clarity and make sense of otherwise complex and ambiguous situations. These "light bulb" moments provide the spark of inspiration that ignites an individual's drive and motivation. The CTM Methodology describes the approach leaders take to achieve guided discovery learning, and guided discovery learning is how the military develops transformational leaders.

The Leader as the Coach

As the coach, leaders facilitate discovery. They close the gap between personal confidence and professional potential. Leaders build authentic connections with the members of their team. We discussed the strategy to build trusted relationships through vulnerability as the foundation in the Hierarchy of

Organizational Agility. Building trust is one example where your vulnerability is an asset. Intimacy and trust are essential to be a successful coach.

Leaders empower individuals to set goals and determine the best path to achieve those goals. This requires introspection and self-awareness, two objectives ideally suited for coaching. As the coach, you increase clarity through a combination of the following: (1) asking open ended questions, (2) sharing multiple perspectives, (3) asking scaling questions, (4) conducting a cause and effect analysis, (5) showing compassion through setbacks, and (6) providing positive reinforcement.[99] Coaches burn off the fog by challenging assumptions, limiting beliefs, flawed reasoning, and self-doubt. Through this application of positive psychology, they widen the aperture of possibilities.

The leader as coach can harness intrinsic forms of motivation. Through one-on-one engagements, they help individuals recognize their personal values and purpose and align those individual qualities with team objectives to achieve shared outcomes. This is how leaders tap into intrinsic forms of motivation to inspire greater levels of performance and organizational citizenship behaviors. This is how they align that intrinsic drive with the confidence and commitment for higher levels of achievement.

Leader as the Teacher

Coaching alone is not enough. At some point, ambition reaches the limit of one's competence. For example, you can "want" to solve a difficult calculus problem all day long, but if you don't know the math, you're wasting your time. Learning expands individual skills and capabilities. Leaders teach based on their own knowledge and experience, and they also champion the practice of intentional competence. Leaders teach subordinates through their example, by supporting external learning opportunities, and by providing candid development feedback during performance counseling sessions.

Leaders are always on display. Therefore, the best opportunity to teach others is through your own example. What you do as a leader sets the standard for behavior in the organization. If you work sixteen hours a day, your team will believe that neglecting their families and working sixteen hours a day is the accepted standard. If you demonstrate resilience and a healthy work-life balance, so will your team. Through your example, you teach others what constitutes appropriate behavior on the team.

The leader as the teacher advocates for lifelong learning. Education, training, and development - both personal and professional - are integrated into the job responsibilities for every member of your team. When you make learning a priority, you encourage members of your team to do the same. You'll know when you've made enough of an investment when you begin to feel an impact on operations. This investment might be painful to the business, but making it on the front end will make your employees more productive and capable in the long run.

Leaders use performance counseling sessions to reinforce the importance of growth and develop strategies for learning. Evaluate employees on their commitment to learning as much as you evaluate their performance on the job. Encourage ambitious learning objectives and hold them accountable to their goals. Make sure that you also acknowledge and celebrate their achievements. Success in the VUCA reality requires a growth mindset. When you increase capabilities through learning and capacity through resilience, you become more adaptive and responsive to unforeseen challenges.

Our modern reality suggests that today's capabilities will be insufficient to meet tomorrow's challenges. Expanding capacity and capability through resilient, adaptive, and dependable leaders on an individual level empowers the potential for the team to seize creative and innovative opportunities at the organizational level. Through teaching, you inspire the members of your team with the will, the stamina, and the aptitude necessary to thrive and win.

Leader as Mentor

The mentor experience is one of the most endearing aspects of the military journey. Most military officers would describe their role as a mentor as the most important and fulfilling responsibility as a leader. These same officers would also describe the experience of working with a mentor as transformational to their personal and professional development.

Mentorship is the voluntary developmental relationship that exists between a person of greater experience and a person of lesser experience and is characterized by mutual **trust** and **respect**. A mentor is a leader who assists personal and professional development by helping a mentee clarify personal, professional, and career goals and develop actions to improve attributes, skills, and competencies. A mentee is the individual receiving mentorship. Individuals are encouraged to participate in mentoring as a voluntary experience. Age or seniority is not a prerequisite for mentor relationships. A junior individual may mentor someone senior to them based on experience or specialized knowledge as a subject matter expert.[100]

To understand mentorship, let's explore some roles and responsibilities, benefits, and strategies to encourage mentorship activities.

Roles and Responsibilities. Your role as a coach and as a mentor are closely related but different. As a coach, the focus is on the individual - their goals, aspirations, and the path to achieve them. **As the mentor, the focus is on your wisdom and experience as the leader.** You provide guidance and advice. You share your personal opinions. The individual is the point of reference through coaching, and you - as the leader - are the point of reference through mentoring.

Your role as a mentor is to provide encouragement and motivation as a credible, trusted confidant and advisor. Start by listening. Understand with compassion. Create a safe environment where you can talk openly about strengths and weaknesses. When appropriate, offer advice about how to overcome obstacles or setbacks. Be the personal confidant and counselor for professional and personal development concerns. As the mentor, tell it to them straight.

Mentor relationships work when both parties reciprocate the same level of energy and commitment. This is why the best mentor relationships are organic. Both parties have to want to invest energy into the relationship. Just as you provide candid feedback to your mentee, they can provide honest appraisals of the organization, policies, or culture from their perspective. Telling it straight goes both ways, and your mentee can help uncover your blind spots. Reciprocating trust, respect, and admiration with the intention for personal and professional development is what distinguishes the mentor relationship from the normal interaction between managers and direct reports.

Benefits. Mentor relationships transcend the power dynamics of the company organizational chart. As such, they provide a means to tap into a person's intrinsic drive. Mentors set an example for the kind of leader that others aspire to become. Mentor relationships also expose junior leaders to the challenges that come with positions of increasing authority and responsibility. They get to see the context and reasons why certain decisions are made. When you expose mentees to the bigger picture, they get a better appreciation and understanding for how their personal contribution contributes to the team effort.

Your organization benefits from effective mentorship. Mentors inspire deeper levels of commitment and higher levels of performance. Employees are more likely to take risks under the guidance and direction of a mentor. The nature of these relationships allows mentors to put their personal stamp on the development of future leaders for the organization - and beyond. The impact of mentor experiences will transcend the immediate job. The development experience provides the mentor satisfaction and validation, the mentee personalized guidance, and the organization a committed workforce based on trusted relationships. Everyone wins when leaders act as mentors.

Strategies. As mentioned earlier, mentorship works best as an organic process. Top-down policies are problematic because effective mentor relationships are based on qualities the organization doesn't control - admiration, trust, and respect. These are human qualities of interpersonal relationships. You can't force them.

Effective mentor engagements require professional relationships based on personal connections. People connect with people - not title, position, or authority. As a mentor, you must be genuine and relatable. Because leaders are always on display, your employees aren't just paying attention to how you do your job, they are paying attention to how you live your life. If you are successful in the office but miserable at home, you are going to have a hard time finding an audience for your wisdom and guidance as a mentor. Employees want to have it all. Nobody really wants to settle. So, if you can't demonstrate how to do both, they will find someone who can.

This means that you should strive to be your best self. It doesn't mean that you need to be perfect. Setbacks make you human. Fallibility is in our nature. Sharing your vulnerability makes you relatable. The challenges you've endured in your life provide a means for personal, authentic connections. For example, sharing the details of a mental health challenge can inspire others to seek mental health support. Rebounding from failure provides hope to others currently experiencing a similar setback. Your vulnerability isn't a weakness. When it comes to building trusting relationships, it is your greatest strength.

Mentor relationships require leaders to be present, supportive, and available. Being present means active listening. You have to pay attention to what is being said and also what is not being said. Being supportive requires a positive attitude with enthusiasm when things go well and constructive feedback when they don't. Being available means you are accessible when others need you. It goes beyond the standard business hours. Being present, supportive, and available is what makes a mentor relationship credible.

The most important responsibility you have as a coach, teacher, and mentor is to LIVE the example. This means practice what you preach. Set your own ambitious goals and a path to achieve them. Engage in your own self-development through continuous learning and education. Show your team what it is like to live a FULL life by prioritizing your family and taking a genuine interest in what matters most to the people who work for you. As the leader, you are always setting an example - whether you intend to do so or not. You get to choose the standard of leadership in your organization. If you want to develop leaders as coaches, teachers, and mentors, it starts with you.

Transformational Leadership: CTM Methodology Concept Summary

Transformational Leadership is the most engaged and effective approach to leadership in the Full Range Leadership Model. It goes beyond the transactional interactions between managers and direct reports to optimize potential and growth on both a personal and professional level. The military's approach to leader development focuses on guided discovery learning - which is an application of transformational leadership. Leaders facilitate discovery through coaching, promote learning through teaching, and provide guidance by mentoring. You can apply this proven application of transformational leadership through the CTM Methodology.

The CTM Methodology applies to military and nonmilitary organizations alike. As a leader, you act as the primary coach, teacher, and mentor. Your specific approach depends on the development needs in your team. Some people need coaching to close the gap between confidence and potential. Others need teaching to attain new knowledge and skills. Still others require a mentor for advice and guidance during uncertain, challenging times. Through your example, you set the standard for developing leaders throughout your organization.

Transformational Leadership: Considerations for Applying the CTM Methodology

The following questions provide a method to assess strengths and potential areas of growth to apply the CTM Methodology:

- How does your organization apply the concepts of individualized consideration, inspirational motivation, idealized influence, and intellectual stimulation from the theory of transformational leadership?

- How do your leaders coach you on your goals (both personal and professional) and your strategies to achieve those goals?

- What is the level of investment your organization makes for lifelong learning to expand the capacity and capability to do more?

- Who in your organization do you see as a mentor? Who within your organization values your insight as a mentor?

- How would you describe the example your leaders set for the organization?

10 | YOUR LEADERSHIP MOMENT

A true leader has the confidence to stand alone, the courage to make tough decisions, and the compassion to listen to the needs of others. He does not set out to be a leader, but becomes one by the equality of his actions and the integrity of his intent.

- Douglas MacArthur

Are you ready for the leadership moment? If you hesitate to answer, you just might be. You can't predict what that moment will be like, but you'll know it when it happens. You'll be scared. You won't have all the answers. Leadership is a choice, and nobody said it was going to be easy.

When I stood to face the crowd in the command center on that fateful day in Kandahar, I wanted nothing more than to *not* be in that situation. It's hard to be a source of strength for others in your most vulnerable moment. True leadership isn't a privilege. It's a burden.

I learned from that event. I would return to Afghanistan during the surge in combat operations a year later. When I did, my scope of responsibility increased. So did the intensity of the fighting. I am sorry to say that I made several more trips to the morgue. I didn't think it was possible, but each trip got progressively worse. Each time I got better because I had to. My role was to do this unpleasant work so that others didn't have to.

I was blessed with great commanders during each of my deployments, but at some point, everyone has to choose whether or not to own their responsibility and step into that leadership moment. I did my part so that the commander could focus his attention on the ongoing fight. That's how you bring more people home to their families at the end of the deployment. I would understand the burden of that responsibility when I became a battalion commander myself. When everyone elevates their game, your team can persevere and win through any crisis. Inspire others to make the necessary sacrifice and commitment for the sake of the team, and in the process, you just might reach the upper limit of your collective potential.

I can't tell you what your leadership moment will look like. What we've outlined in this book is a way for you and your team to be prepared when it happens. The ADAPT Framework is the bridge. It applies the best practices from the military experience to address leadership challenges in any organization and any environment. It starts with a strong core of values and purpose. These qualities keep the entire team grounded in the storm of uncertainty. People turn to leaders for clarity during a crisis, and leaders find clarity in their sense of values and purpose.

Through every leadership moment in my military career, I felt the burden of others placing their faith in me. In truth, I had to place my faith in them. Being a "team" wasn't enough. We needed something stronger than that. We needed to be like a family. By developing a culture of camaraderie, we could draw inspiration from each other through good times and bad.

We leveraged this trust and combined it with intentional competence as a foundation for organizational agility. We described a vision of what winning looked like and encouraged junior leaders to seek out opportunities to make it happen. We exercised an inclusive process to critically analyze problems and develop creative, flexible solutions. We accepted mistakes and learned from them. We were committed to our people and accepted the risk in doing so, because we wanted them to find opportunities, seize the initiative, and create the necessary advantage to win.

The objective of our process wasn't to control but to empower. We established routines - a cadence - to our systems to provide a measure of predictability in otherwise unpredictable situations. We streamlined the mechanisms for collaboration, communication, and sharing information to keep people focused on identifying opportunities while mitigating vulnerabilities.

Finally, we did all this through personal engagements as a coach, teacher, and mentor. The goal was to unleash individual potential to inspire, learn, and grow. Interestingly enough, when you work to inspire others, you inspire yourself. When your people hunger to learn, you learn. When you commit to the growth of others, you grow as well. Your commitment ignites a passion for people to become better versions of themselves. Likewise, you draw from their energy to become the best version of yourself.

Better people become the best doctors, lawyers, engineers, sales representatives, politicians, athletes, and soldiers. When you commit to the people, you gain confidence in their competence. You expand the capacity and capability of the team to do more. Your team becomes more resilient, adaptive, and dependable to anticipate contingencies, shape them in a proactive way to create an advantage, and seize opportunities to win.

It starts with you. You have to make a choice. You can stay seated in the crowd and follow the numbers, or you can stand. You can choose to lead. Yes, you'll be scared. No, you won't have all the answers. You need the right amount of confidence, competence, and commitment for others to place their faith in you. That requires the right mix of courage and vulnerability. Having the courage to stand and inspire others to rise to their feet when every impulse is to remain seated is the only measure of effective leadership. Protect your people. Be present through the challenge. Invest all of your energy to inspire and guide them. That's the spendthrift moral act. True leadership is about the people. Make them your mission. They achieve the results. Choose to lead, and when you do, you inspire the team with the best chance to win.

ENDNOTES

1. Anton Myrer, *Once an Eagle* (New York: Harper Perennial, 2002), 1288.

2. Pierre Gurdjian, Thomas Halbeisen, and Kevin Lane, "Why Leadership-Development Programs Fail," McKinsey & Company, February 22, 2019, https://www.mckinsey.com/featured-insights/leadership/why-leadership-development-programs-fail.

3. Mihnea Moldoveanu and Das Narayandas, "The Future of Leadership Development," *Harvard Business Review*, November 9, 2020, https://hbr.org/2019/03/the-future-of-leadership-development.

4. Nadya Zhexembayeva, "3 Things You're Getting Wrong About Organizational Change," *Harvard Business Review*, June 9, 2020, https://hbr.org/2020/06/3-things-youre-getting-wrong-about-organizational-change.

5. Defense Manpower Data Center, Number of Military and DoD Appropriated Fund (APF) Civilian Personnel Permanently Assigned, DRS 103763, (Washington, D.C.: Department of Defense, September 30, 2020), https://www.dmdc.osd.mil/appj/dwp/dwp_reports.jsp.

6. "Research Starters: US Military by the Numbers: The National WWII Museum: New Orleans," The National WWII Museum | New Orleans, accessed April 5, 2021, https://www.nationalww2museum.org/students-teachers/student-resources/research-starters/research-starters-us-military-numbers.

7. Sharon R. Cohany, "Labor Force Status of Vietnam-Era Veterans : Monthly Labor Review," U.S. Bureau of Labor Statistics (U.S. Bureau of Labor Statistics, February 1, 1987), https://www.bls.gov/opub/mlr/1987/article/labor-force-status-of-vietnam-era-veterans.htm, 13.

8. Bureau of Labor Statistics, "Employment Situation of Veterans - 2019," news release no. USDL-20-0452, March 19, 2020, https://www.bls.gov/news.release/pdf/vet.pdf.

9. Kristen Bialik, "5 Facts about U.S. Veterans," Pew Research Center, May 30, 2020, https://www.pewresearch.org/fact-tank/2017/11/10/the-changing-face-of-americas-veteran-population/.

10. Harry Enten, "Congress' Approval Rating Hasn't Hit 30% in 10 Years. That's a Record. - CNN Politics," CNN, June 1, 2019, https://www.cnn.com/2019/06/01/politics/poll-of-the-week-congress-approval-rating/index.html.

11. Kimberly Weisul, "Where Are All the Missing Veteran-Owned Businesses?," Inc.com, October 3, 2016, https://www.inc.com/magazine/201610/kimberly-weisul/missing-veteran-owned-businesses.html.

12. Ray Fisman, "CEOs Who Served in the Military Are More Honest. But They Make Their Companies Less Money," *Slate Magazine*, May 25, 2012, https://slate.com/business/2012/05/ceos-who-served-in-the-military-are-they-more-honest.html.

13. Ibid.

14. Mark Emmons, "Key Statistics about Millennials in the Workplace," Dynamic Signal, accessed June 14, 2020, https://dynamicsignal.com/2018/10/09/key-statistics-millennials-in-the-workplace/.

15. Stephen M. R. Covey and Rebecca R. Merrill, *The Speed of Trust: the One Thing That Changes Everything* (New York, NY: Free Press, 2018), 11.

16. Marcel Schwantes, "A New Study Reveals 70 Percent of Workers Say They Are Actively Looking for a New Job. Here's the Reason in 5 Words," Inc.com, December 4, 2018, https://www.inc.com/marcel-schwantes/a-new-study-reveals-70-percent-of-workers-say-they-are-actively-looking-for-a-new-job-heres-reason-in-5-words.html.

17. Amy Adkins, "Millennials: The Job-Hopping Generation," Gallup.com, April 17, 2020, https://www.gallup.com/workplace/236474/millennials-job-hopping-generation.aspx.

18. Katherine Bell and Tom Kolditz, "What Business Leaders Can Learn from Today's Military," February 20, 2009, podcast, transcript, 13:59, https://hbr.org/podcast/2009/02/what-business-leaders-can-lear.

19. Klaus Schwab, *The Fourth Industrial Revolution*, (New York, Crown Publishing Group, 2016).

20. Munozovepi Gwata, "To Flourish in the Fourth Industrial Revolution, We Need to Rethink These 3 Things," World Economic Forum, August 05, 2019, https://www.weforum.org/agenda/2019/08/fourth-industrial-revolution-education/.

21. Stephanie Schomer, "He Asked His Team How to Avoid Layoffs. Their Response Thrilled Him, *Entrepreneur*, December 02, 2020, https://www.entrepreneur.com/article/359946.

22. Anders Melin, "CEOs Cut Millions of Jobs amid Coronavirus Yet Keep Their Lofty Bonuses," Business, *Los Angeles Times*, May 15, 2020, https://www.latimes.com/business/story/2020-05-15/ceos-cut-millions-of-jobs-keep-big-bonuses.

23. Globoforce, *2016 SHRM/Globoforce Employee Recognition Survey: Employee Experience as a Business Driver*, 2017, http://go.globoforce.com/rs/862-JIQ-698/images/2017_EmployeeExperienceAsBusinessDriver.pdf.

24. Ibid.

25. Randy Conley, "Infographic: New Managers Aren't Getting The Training They Need to Succeed," Leading with Trust, October 9, 2016,

https://leadingwithtrust.com/2016/10/09/infographic-new-managers-arent-getting-the-training-they-need-to-succeed/.

26. Peter Manzo, "Fail Faster, Succeed Sooner (SSIR)," Stanford Social Innovation Review: Informing and Inspiring Leaders of Social Change, September 23, 2008, https://ssir.org/articles/entry/fail_faster_succeed_sooner.

27. Lauren Garris, "Being Smart about Emotional Intelligence," HR Professional Now - HR Professional Now, accessed April 5, 2021, http://hrprofessionalnow.ca/talent-management/223-being-smart-about-emotional-intelligence.

28. Joshua Freedman, "Workplace Vitality Research: Trends in Leadership • Six Seconds," Six Seconds, December 4, 2020, https://www.6seconds.org/2020/07/05/workplace-vitality-research/.

29. Department of the Army, Headquarters, *ADP 6-22: Army Leadership and the Profession* (Washington, D.C.: US Army, November 25, 2019), 1-15.

30. Daniel Goleman, "Leadership That Gets Results," *Harvard Business Review*, March 2000, https://hbr.org/2000/03/leadership-that-gets-results. The definitions for each of the Emotional Intelligence Traits used in Figures 1 through 4 are direct quotations from the same graphic *Emotional Intelligence: A Primer*. The notes for the Army Leadership Requirements Model in Figures 1 through 4 are also direct quotations that are annotated separately because they come from different parts of the manual. Direct quotations were used in Figures 1 through 4 to showcase the similarity between the competencies for emotional intelligence and the attributes and competencies of the Army Leadership Model.

31. Department of the Army, *Army Leadership*, 4-2.

32. Ibid., 6-3.

33. Ibid., 3-1.

34. Ibid., 2-10.

35. Ibid., 4-3.

36. Ibid., 2-11.

37. Ibid., Table 5-4.

38. Ibid., Table 4-1.

39. Ibid., Table 5-4.

40. Ibid., 4-1.

41. Ibid., 2-8.

42. Ibid., Table 5-3.

43. Ibid., 2-8.

44. Ibid., Table 5-1.

45. Ibid., 5-3.

46. Department of the Army, Headquarters, *FM 6-22: Leader Development* (Washington, D.C.: US Army, 2015), 7-46.

47. Department of the Army, *Army Leadership*, Table 5-5.

48. Ibid., 4-2.

49. Ibid., 6-6.

50. Ibid., Table 5-2.

51. Ibid., Table 6-2.

52. Patrick M. Lencioni, "Make Your Values Mean Something," *Harvard Business Review*, July 2002, https://hbr.org/2002/07/make-your-values-mean-something.

53. Ken Silverstein, "Enron, Ethics and Today's Corporate Values," *Forbes*, May 14, 2003, https://www.forbes.com/sites/kensilverstein/2013/05/14/enron-ethics-and-todays-corporate-values/?sh=621cff0d5ab8.

54. Richard M. Ryan and Edward L. Deci, "Self-Determination Theory and the Facilitation of Intrinsic Motivation, Social Development, and Well-Being," *American Psychologist*, 55, no. 1 (2000): 70.

55. Ibid., 69.

56. Center for the Army Profession and Ethic, *The Army's Framework for Character Development*, (Fort Leavenworth, KS: Combined Arms Center, 2017): 3. The metaphor in this white paper focuses on the apples and barrels, and we expanded this comparison to include "the store.:

57. Ibid., 5. The Character Alignment Methodology is an adaptation of the graphic on this page.

58. Ryan and Deci, "Self-Determination Theory," 68.

59. Ibid., 71. This chart utilizes the steps and behavioral processes found in *Figure 1. The Self-Determination Continuum Showing Types of Motivation With Their Regulatory Styles, Loci of Causality, and Corresponding Processes*.

60. Department of the Army, Headquarters, *AR 600-20: Army Command Policy* (Washington D.C.: US Army, 2014), 6.

61. Brené Brown, *Rising Strong: The Reckoning. The Rumble. The Revolution*, (New York: Spiegel & Grau, 2015), 4.

62. Charles Duhigg, "What Google Learned From Its Quest to Build the Perfect Team," The New York Times Magazine, *The New York Times*, February 25, 2016, https://www.nytimes.com/2016/02/28/magazine/what-google-learned-from-its-quest-to-build-the-perfect-team.html.

63. Brené Brown, *Daring Greatly: How the Courage to Be Vulnerable Transforms the Way We Live, Love, Parent, and Lead*, (New York: Penguin Random House, 2012), 34.

64. Department of the Army, Headquarters, *ADP 6-0: Mission Command* (Washington D.C.: US Army, 2019), 1-3.

65. Ibid., 1-7.

66. Milvio di Bartolomeo, "VUCA Prime – The answer to a VUCA dynamic," Axelos.com, November 7, 2019, https://www.axelos.com/news/blogs/november-2019/vuca-prime-the-answer-to-a-vuca-dynamic.

67. Department of the Army, *Leader Development*, 3-3.

68. Department of the Army, Headquarters, *FM 6-0: Commander and Staff Organization and Operations*, (Washington D.C.: US Army, 2014), 16-1-16-2. This chart was developed from the information from paragraph 16-6.

69. Ibid., 9-14.

70. Department of the Army, *Mission Command*, 1-12.

71. Ibid., 1-14.

72. Ulrich Pidun, Martin Reeves, and Maximilian Schüssler, "Why Do Most Business Ecosystems Fail?," BCG Global, June 22, 2020, https://www.bcg.com/publications/2020/why-do-most-business-ecosystems-fail.

73. Michael Beer, "6 Reasons Your Strategy Isn't Working," *Harvard Business Review*, June 22, 2020, https://hbr.org/2020/06/6-reasons-your-strategy-isnt-working.

74. Department of the Army, *Commander and Staff*, 4-3.

75. Ibid., 9-9.

76. Ibid.

77. Department of the Army, Headquarters, *ADP 5.0: The Operations Process*, (Washington D.C.: US Army, 2019), 1-12.

78. Department of the Army, *Commander and Staff*, 4-4.

79. Ibid.

80. Ibid.

81. Ibid., 15-2.

82. Ibid., 9-21.

83. Ibid., 9-26

84. Ibid., 9-41.

85. Department of the Army, *Commander and Staff*, 3-7.

86. Department of the Army, Headquarters, *Risk Management*, (Washington D.C.: US Army, 2014), 1-1.

87. Ibid., 1-3.

88. Ibid., 1-6.

89. Department of the Army, *Commander and Staff*, 7-2.

90. Bernard M. Bass and Bruce J. Avolio, *Improving Organizational Effectiveness: through Transformational Leadership* (Thousand Oaks, CA: Sage, 2000), 32-33.

91. Hira Khan, Maryam Rehmat, Tahira Hassan Butt, Saira Farooqi, and Javaria Asim, "Impact of Transformational Leadership on Work Performance, Burnout and Social Loafing: a

Mediation Model," *Future Business Journal* 6, no. 1 (2020), https://doi.org/10.1186/s43093-020-00043-8.

92. Edward L. Deci, Richard Koestner, and Richard M. Ryan, "A Meta-Analytic Review of Experiments Examining the Effects of Extrinsic Rewards on Intrinsic Motivation," *Psychological Bulletin* 125, no. 6 (1999): pp. 627-668, https://doi.org/10.1037/0033-2909.125.6.627.

93. Bass and Avolio, *Improving Organizational*, 3.

94. Ibid., 3-4. This reference provided the material for the Four I's in Figure 25.

95. Ibid., 12.

96. Ashley DiFranza, "Transformational Leadership: How to Inspire Innovation in the Workplace," Northeastern University Graduate Programs, March 16, 2021, https://www.northeastern.edu/graduate/blog/transformational-leadership/.

97. Bass and Avolio, *Improving Organizational*, 28.

98. Department of the Army, *Leader Development*, 3-22.

99. Ibid.

100. Ibid., 3-17.

ACKNOWLEDGEMENTS

From Jason Roncoroni:

I'd like to thank my wife, partner, and best friend, Jill who always pushes me to be the best version of myself. To Aidan and Everett, may I inspire the example for you to achieve your fullest potential. To my parents, Linda and Ed, who I have only recently understood the selfless sacrifice you made for the wellbeing of others. I want to thank the people who took the time to provide feedback for this work including Ian Fuller, Margaret Kurtts, Machim McHargue. To the commanders who leaned into your leadership moments — Tommy Stauss, Bill Gayler, and John Kline — thank you for being the example I needed to step into those defining moments of leadership. Finally, I'd like to thank my co-author and business partner, Zebrina Warner, for her collaboration, vision, and friendship to improve our society by inspiring the next generation's leaders.

From Zebrina Warner:

My biggest thanks goes to my partner, greatest supporter, and rock, Chad. His unconditional love for our whole family is the light we all need to succeed in our lives. To my boys, Eli and Samuel, you both teach me more about life and myself than anyone. To my parents, Richard and Vera, who taught me the value of leading from the heart and how kindness prevails in all situations - good and bad. A special thanks and remembrance of the mentors I've had in my life, Bill Powell, David Wood, and Clay Whybark. All of whom saw greatness in me, pushed me hard, and celebrated my wins with me. Thank you to Davis Ellison for feedback on the book, and Tushar Varma, Founder of Astra, for all the graphics of the book. Last but not least, I want to thank Jason Roncoroni, my partner, creative genius, and friend, for being an awesome human being and leader.

Made in the USA
Coppell, TX
10 November 2021

65533024R00095